TABLEAU FUNCTIONS DICTIONARY

Exploring the Language of Data Analysis

Kiet Huynh

Table of Contents

Introduction

Welcome to "Tableau Functions Dictionary: Exploring the Language of Data Analysis." In this book, we'll guide you through the fascinating world of data analysis and the utilization of Tableau functions. You can expect concrete examples and detailed step-by-step instructions that will equip you with practical skills. Join us on this journey as we dive into the art of turning data into meaningful insights.

What You Can Expect

- A comprehensive dictionary of Tableau functions: This book provides you with a curated collection of Tableau functions, each meticulously explained with practical examples.

- Real-world applications: We go beyond the theoretical and provide you with real-world scenarios where these functions shine, enabling you to apply your newfound knowledge effectively.

- Step-by-step tutorials: Our approach is hands-on. You'll find step-by-step tutorials that guide you through the process of using these functions, making the learning experience interactive and engaging.

"Tableau Functions Dictionary: Exploring the Language of Data Analysis" is more than just a reference book; it's a journey to becoming a proficient data communicator. Join us on this exploration of the language of data analysis and take your data skills to new heights.

Welcome to the world of Tableau functions, where data becomes your canvas, and insights are your masterpiece.

Tableau vs. Power BI: A Comparative Analysis

Data visualization and business intelligence tools have become essential for organizations to make data-driven decisions and gain insights from their data. Two popular choices in this space are Tableau and Power BI, each with its unique features and characteristics. In this analysis, we'll explore the key differences and similarities between Tableau and Power BI to help you decide which one is better suited for your specific needs.

1. User Interface and Ease of Use:

- **Tableau:** Tableau offers a flexible and intuitive drag-and-drop interface, which is known for its ease of use. Users can quickly create visually appealing dashboards without extensive technical knowledge.

- **Power BI:** Power BI, designed by Microsoft, has a more user-friendly interface, especially for individuals already familiar with other Microsoft products. It's known for its simplicity and integration with Office 365 tools.

2. Data Sources and Connectivity:

- **Tableau:** Tableau supports a wide range of data sources, from spreadsheets to cloud databases. It's well-regarded for its data connectivity capabilities, making it an excellent choice for organizations with diverse data sources.

- **Power BI:** Power BI also supports various data sources and provides seamless integration with other Microsoft products, such as Azure, Excel, and SQL Server.

3. Data Visualization Capabilities:

- **Tableau:** Tableau is renowned for its extensive data visualization capabilities. It offers a plethora of charts, graphs, and mapping options. Users can create complex visualizations, and it's often the preferred choice for more data-centric organizations.

- **Power BI:** Power BI excels in creating visually appealing and interactive reports. It may have a slightly steeper learning curve for creating complex visualizations, but it's perfect for organizations looking for user-friendly reports.

4. Pricing and Licensing:

- **Tableau:** Tableau's licensing structure can be cost-prohibitive for small and medium-sized businesses. It offers Tableau Desktop for report creation and Tableau Server for sharing, which adds to the cost.

- **Power BI:** Power BI offers a free version with limitations, making it more accessible to small businesses. The Pro and Premium versions offer advanced features but come at a fraction of the cost of Tableau.

5. Collaboration and Sharing:

- **Tableau:** Tableau Server and Tableau Online facilitate collaboration and sharing among users. It allows publishing and sharing reports, granting permissions, and accessing content via the web.

- **Power BI:** Power BI offers collaboration through sharing workspaces and dashboards. Users can collaborate in real-time and share reports via the web, making it a strong contender in this aspect.

6. Data Modeling and ETL:

- **Tableau:** Tableau provides limited data modeling capabilities. It relies on pre-modeled data sources. Data transformation and cleansing must typically be done outside of Tableau.

- **Power BI:** Power BI excels in data modeling and ETL (Extract, Transform, Load) capabilities. Its Power Query and Power Pivot tools allow users to perform data transformations and create relationships between tables.

7. Mobile Capabilities:

- **Tableau:** Tableau offers mobile apps for iOS and Android devices, ensuring access to reports and dashboards on the go.

- **Power BI:** Power BI Mobile also provides apps for mobile access. It benefits from Microsoft's expertise in mobile technology.

Conclusion:

The choice between Tableau and Power BI ultimately depends on your specific needs, budget, and preferences. Tableau is favored for its data visualization capabilities, data connectivity, and data source support, making it suitable for data-centric organizations. Power BI, with its user-friendly interface and lower cost, is an excellent option for businesses that want to quickly get started with business intelligence and reporting. Both tools are powerful and can deliver valuable insights when used effectively, so the decision comes down to your specific use case and organizational requirements.

I.
Aggregation Functions

1.1 SUM

Description:

The SUM function in Tableau is used to calculate the sum of a specified numeric field or expression in a dataset. It is a common aggregation function that provides the total value of the selected field or expression across the data rows that meet the defined criteria.

Syntax:

The syntax for the SUM function is as follows:

```
SUM(expression)
```

- `expression`: This is the field or expression for which you want to calculate the sum. It can be a numeric field, a calculation, or an aggregation.

Example Usage:

Suppose you have a dataset containing sales data for a retail store, and you want to calculate the total sales for a specific product category. You can use the SUM function as follows:

```tableau
SUM(IF [Category] = 'Electronics' THEN [Sales] END)
```

- In this example, we are using an IF statement to filter the data for the 'Electronics' category.

- The SUM function then calculates the sum of sales values for this category.

Tips:

1. When using the SUM function, make sure the field or expression you specify is numeric. If you apply SUM to a non-numeric field, it will result in an error.

2. You can use the SUM function in combination with other functions and conditional statements to perform more complex calculations, such as calculating conditional sums for specific categories or time periods.

Note: This is a simplified example, and the actual usage of the SUM function may vary depending on the complexity of your data and analysis requirements.

1.2 AVG

Description:

The AVG function in Tableau is used to calculate the average or mean value of a specified numeric field or expression in a dataset. It provides the arithmetic mean of the selected field's values, which is the sum of values divided by the count of values.

Syntax:

The syntax for the AVG function is as follows:

```
AVG(expression)
```

- `expression`: This is the field or expression for which you want to calculate the average. It must be a numeric field, calculation, or aggregation.

Example Usage:

Let's consider a dataset containing test scores for students. You want to find the average test score. You can use the AVG function as follows:

```tableau
AVG([Test Score])
```

- In this example, the AVG function takes the 'Test Score' field as an argument.

- It calculates the average of all test scores in the dataset.

Tips:

1. Ensure that the field or expression you use with the AVG function is numeric. If it's not a numeric field, Tableau will generate an error.

2. AVG is often used in combination with other functions or calculations, such as filtering data to find the average of a specific category or time period.

3. Be cautious when using the AVG function with fields that may contain NULL values. To handle NULL values appropriately, you may need to use the IFNULL function or other techniques to ensure accurate averages.

Note: The actual application of the AVG function can be more complex depending on your specific data analysis needs and the types of visualizations you are creating.

1.3 MIN

Description:

The MIN function in Tableau is used to find the minimum (smallest) value in a specified numeric field or expression in a dataset. It helps identify the lowest numeric value within the given dataset, which can be valuable in data analysis and visualization.

Syntax:

The syntax for the MIN function is as follows:

```
MIN(expression)
```

- `expression`: This is the field or expression for which you want to find the minimum value. It must be a numeric field, calculation, or aggregation.

Example Usage:

Let's consider a dataset containing product prices, and you want to determine the lowest price among all products. You can use the MIN function as follows:

```tableau
MIN([Product Price])
```

- In this example, the MIN function takes the 'Product Price' field as an argument.
- It evaluates and identifies the product with the lowest price.

Tips:

1. Ensure that the field or expression you use with the MIN function is numeric. Attempting to use MIN on a non-numeric field will result in an error.

2. MIN can be combined with other functions or filters to find the minimum value within a subset of your data. For instance, you might find the minimum price within a specific product category.

3. Keep in mind that the MIN function considers NULL values as the lowest value. If NULL values are present in your dataset, consider handling them appropriately using IFNULL or ISNULL functions.

Note: The application of the MIN function can vary depending on your data analysis requirements and the visualization you are creating.

1.4 MAX

Description:

The MAX function in Tableau is used to find the maximum (largest) value in a specified numeric field or expression in a dataset. It helps identify the highest numeric value within the given dataset, which can be valuable for data analysis and visualization.

Syntax:

The syntax for the MAX function is as follows:

```
MAX(expression)
```

- `expression`: This is the field or expression for which you want to find the maximum value. It must be a numeric field, calculation, or aggregation.

Example Usage:

Let's consider a dataset containing the population of cities, and you want to determine the city with the highest population. You can use the MAX function as follows:

```tableau
MAX([Population])
```

- In this example, the MAX function takes the 'Population' field as an argument.

- It evaluates and identifies the city with the highest population.

Tips:

1. Ensure that the field or expression you use with the MAX function is numeric. Attempting to use MAX on a non-numeric field will result in an error.

2. MAX can be combined with other functions or filters to find the maximum value within a subset of your data. For example, you might find the maximum population within a specific region or country.

3. Be aware that the MAX function considers NULL values as the highest value. If NULL values are present in your dataset, consider handling them appropriately using IFNULL or ISNULL functions.

Note: The application of the MAX function can vary based on your specific data analysis needs and the type of visualization you are creating.

1.5 COUNT

Description:

The COUNT function in Tableau is used to count the number of non-null values in a specified field. It provides a count of records or rows within a dataset that meet a certain condition. COUNT is commonly used to determine the frequency or occurrence of specific data values.

Syntax:

The syntax for the COUNT function is as follows:

```
```

COUNT(expression)

```
```

- `expression`: This is the field or expression for which you want to count the non-null values. It can be any field, calculation, or aggregation.

Example Usage:

Suppose you have a dataset of customer orders and you want to count the number of orders placed by each customer. You can use the COUNT function as follows:

```tableau
COUNTD([Order ID])
```

- In this example, the COUNT function counts the number of unique 'Order ID' values, representing the distinct orders placed by each customer.

Explanation of the Code:

- COUNTD is used for counting distinct values. It counts the unique occurrences of 'Order ID.'

- The result is a count of distinct orders placed by customers.

Tips:

1. COUNT can be used to count non-null values within a specific field or expression. It doesn't count NULL values.

2. For counting unique or distinct values, use COUNTD instead of COUNT.

3. COUNT can also be combined with other functions and filters to count values that meet specific conditions, such as counting orders for a specific product category.

Note: The application of the COUNT function can vary based on your specific data analysis requirements and the type of visualization you are creating.

1.6 COUNTD

Description:

The COUNTD function in Tableau is used to count the number of distinct or unique values in a specified field or expression. It provides a count of unique occurrences, ignoring duplicate values. COUNTD is particularly useful when you want to determine the number of different items within a dataset.

Syntax:

The syntax for the COUNTD function is as follows:

```
COUNTD(expression)
```

- `expression`: This is the field or expression for which you want to count the distinct values. It can be any field, calculation, or aggregation.

Example Usage:

Suppose you have a dataset of customer orders, and you want to count the number of unique products ordered by each customer. You can use the COUNTD function as follows:

```tableau
COUNTD([Product Name])
```

- In this example, the COUNTD function counts the number of distinct 'Product Name' values, representing the unique products ordered by each customer.

Explanation of the Code:

- COUNTD is used for counting distinct values.

- The expression `[Product Name]` is the field for which unique values are counted.

- The result is the count of distinct product names ordered by customers.

Tips:

1. COUNTD is ideal for counting unique values within a field or expression. It disregards duplicate values and NULL values.

2. Use COUNTD when you want to count distinct occurrences, such as counting unique customers, products, or categories.

3. COUNTD can also be used in combination with other functions and filters to count unique values that meet specific conditions, such as counting unique customers in a certain region.

Note: The application of the COUNTD function may vary depending on your specific data analysis needs and the type of visualization you are creating.

Description:

The MEDIAN function in Tableau is used to calculate the median value of a specified numeric field or expression in a dataset. The median is the middle value when a set of values is ordered from lowest to highest. It is a robust measure of central tendency, making it less sensitive to extreme values compared to the mean (average).

Syntax:

The syntax for the MEDIAN function is as follows:

```
MEDIAN(expression)
```

- `expression`: This is the field or expression for which you want to calculate the median. It must be a numeric field, calculation, or aggregation.

Example Usage:

Suppose you have a dataset containing the scores of students in a test, and you want to find the median score. You can use the MEDIAN function as follows:

```tableau
MEDIAN([Test Score])
```

- In this example, the MEDIAN function takes the 'Test Score' field as an argument.

- It calculates the median score, which is the middle value when all the test scores are ordered from lowest to highest.

Explanation of the Code:

- The MEDIAN function calculates the median value of the 'Test Score' field.

- It orders the test scores in ascending order and finds the middle value. If there is an even number of values, the median is the average of the two middle values.

Tips:

1. MEDIAN is a useful measure when you want to understand the central tendency of your data without being heavily influenced by extreme values.

2. Ensure that the field or expression you use with the MEDIAN function is numeric. Attempting to use MEDIAN on a non-numeric field will result in an error.

3. The MEDIAN function is robust and often a better choice than the mean when dealing with datasets that may have outliers or skewed distributions.

Note: The application of the MEDIAN function can vary depending on your specific data analysis requirements and the type of visualization you are creating.

1.8 PERCENTILE

Description:

The PERCENTILE function in Tableau is used to calculate the value at a specified percentile within a numeric field or expression in a dataset. Percentiles divide a dataset into hundredths, and the PERCENTILE function helps you find the value below which a given percentage of the data falls. It is useful for understanding the distribution and spread of data.

Syntax:

The syntax for the PERCENTILE function is as follows:

```
PERCENTILE(expression, percentile)
```

- `expression`: This is the field or expression for which you want to calculate the percentile. It must be a numeric field, calculation, or aggregation.

- `percentile`: The desired percentile value, expressed as a decimal between 0 and 1.

Example Usage:

Suppose you have a dataset containing the scores of students in a test, and you want to find the 75th percentile score. You can use the PERCENTILE function as follows:

```tableau
PERCENTILE([Test Score], 0.75)
```

- In this example, the PERCENTILE function takes the 'Test Score' field as an argument.

- It calculates the score at the 75th percentile, indicating the value below which 75% of the test scores fall.

Explanation of the Code:

- The PERCENTILE function calculates the value at the specified percentile (75th percentile in this case) of the 'Test Score' field.

- It orders the test scores in ascending order, and then finds the score below which 75% of the scores are located.

Tips:

1. Ensure that the field or expression you use with the PERCENTILE function is numeric. Attempting to use PERCENTILE on a non-numeric field will result in an error.

2. Choose an appropriate percentile value to analyze data distribution. The 50th percentile is the median, the 25th and 75th percentiles represent the interquartile range, and percentiles can be used to identify outliers or extreme values.

3. When working with large datasets, consider using the PERCENTILE_CONT function to calculate percentiles more efficiently.

Note: The application of the PERCENTILE function is valuable for analyzing data distributions and understanding where specific data points fall within a dataset.

1.9 STDDEV

Description:

The STDDEV function in Tableau is used to calculate the standard deviation of a specified numeric field or expression in a dataset. Standard deviation measures the dispersion or spread of data points around the mean (average). It is valuable for understanding the variability and consistency of data.

Syntax:

The syntax for the STDDEV function is as follows:

```
STDDEV(expression)
```

- `expression`: This is the field or expression for which you want to calculate the standard deviation. It must be a numeric field, calculation, or aggregation.

Example Usage:

Suppose you have a dataset containing the daily sales of a retail store, and you want to calculate the standard deviation of daily sales. You can use the STDDEV function as follows:

```tableau
STDDEV([Daily Sales])
```

- In this example, the STDDEV function takes the 'Daily Sales' field as an argument.

- It calculates the standard deviation, which quantifies how much the daily sales values deviate from their mean.

Explanation of the Code:

- The STDDEV function calculates the standard deviation of the 'Daily Sales' field.

- It computes the square root of the average of the squared differences between each daily sales value and the mean of the dataset.

Tips:

1. Standard deviation is a useful measure for understanding the spread of data. A higher standard deviation indicates greater variability, while a lower standard deviation suggests more consistency.

2. Ensure that the field or expression you use with the STDDEV function is numeric. Attempting to use STDDEV on a non-numeric field will result in an error.

3. Standard deviation is sensitive to outliers. If your dataset contains extreme values, consider using the robust version of the standard deviation, which is less affected by outliers.

Note: The application of the STDDEV function is valuable for assessing the consistency and variability of data, which can inform decisions related to data analysis and visualization.

1.10 VARIANCE

Description:

The VARIANCE function in Tableau is used to calculate the variance of a specified numeric field or expression in a dataset. Variance is a measure of how data points deviate from the mean (average) of the dataset. It quantifies the spread and dispersion of data values.

Syntax:

The syntax for the VARIANCE function is as follows:

```

VARIANCE(expression)

```

- `expression`: This is the field or expression for which you want to calculate the variance. It must be a numeric field, calculation, or aggregation.

Example Usage:

Suppose you have a dataset containing the daily temperatures for a month, and you want to calculate the variance in daily temperatures. You can use the VARIANCE function as follows:

```tableau
VARIANCE([Daily Temperature])
```

- In this example, the VARIANCE function takes the 'Daily Temperature' field as an argument.

- It calculates the variance, which measures how much daily temperatures vary from their mean over the month.

Explanation of the Code:

- The VARIANCE function calculates the variance of the 'Daily Temperature' field.

- It computes the average of the squared differences between each daily temperature value and the mean temperature of the month.

Tips:

1. Variance provides insight into the variability of data. A higher variance indicates more spread or dispersion, while a lower variance suggests less variability and more consistency.

2. Ensure that the field or expression you use with the VARIANCE function is numeric. Attempting to use VARIANCE on a non-numeric field will result in an error.

3. Variance is sensitive to outliers, which can significantly affect the result. If your dataset contains extreme values, consider using a robust version of variance, such as the robust variance or the mean absolute deviation.

Note: The VARIANCE function is valuable for understanding the spread and variability of data, making it useful in various data analysis and visualization scenarios.

II.
Logical Functions

2.1 IF

Description:

The IF function in Tableau is a logical function used to perform conditional logic and return different values or outcomes based on a specified condition. It allows you to create custom calculations and expressions by evaluating whether a condition is true or false.

Syntax:

The syntax for the IF function is as follows:

```
IF condition THEN value1 ELSE value2 END
```

- `condition`: This is the logical condition you want to evaluate. If it is true, the function returns `value1`; otherwise, it returns `value2`.

- `value1`: The value to be returned if the `condition` is true.

- `value2`: The value to be returned if the `condition` is false.

Example Usage:

Suppose you have a dataset of student exam scores, and you want to create a calculated field that categorizes students as "Pass" if their score is greater than or equal to 50 and "Fail" if their score is less than 50. You can use the IF function as follows:

```tableau

IF [Score] >= 50 THEN "Pass" ELSE "Fail" END

```

- In this example, the `condition` `[Score] >= 50` is evaluated for each student's score.

- If the condition is true (the score is greater than or equal to 50), the function returns "Pass"; otherwise, it returns "Fail."

Explanation of the Code:

- The IF function checks the `condition` for each row in the dataset.

- If the `condition` is true, "Pass" is returned; otherwise, "Fail" is returned.

Tips:

1. The IF function is useful for creating custom categories, aggregations, or conditional calculations in your data.

2. Ensure that the `condition`, `value1`, and `value2` are appropriate for the specific context of your data analysis or visualization.

3. You can nest IF functions to handle multiple conditions and outcomes, creating more complex logic.

Note: The IF function is a fundamental tool for applying conditional logic in Tableau, allowing you to tailor your analysis and visualizations to specific criteria and scenarios.

2.2 AND

Description:

The AND function in Tableau is a logical function used to combine multiple conditions and determine if all of them are true. It returns a Boolean result, which is true if all conditions are true, and false if any condition is false. The AND function is often used to create more complex conditional logic.

Syntax:

The syntax for the AND function is as follows:

```
AND(condition1, condition2, ...)
```

- `condition1`, `condition2`, etc.: These are the individual logical conditions you want to combine. You can include as many conditions as needed.

Example Usage:

Suppose you have a dataset of employees, and you want to identify employees who are both managers and have more than five years of experience. You can use the AND function as follows:

```tableau
AND([Is Manager] = TRUE, [Years of Experience] > 5)
```

- In this example, the AND function evaluates two conditions:

  - `[Is Manager] = TRUE`: Checks if the employee is a manager.

- `[Years of Experience] > 5`: Checks if the employee has more than five years of experience.

Explanation of the Code:

- The AND function combines the two conditions.

- If both conditions are true for a specific employee, the function returns true; otherwise, it returns false.

Tips:

1. The AND function is particularly useful when you want to apply multiple criteria to filter or categorize data.

2. Ensure that the individual conditions are structured correctly and evaluate the desired aspects of your data.

3. You can nest AND functions within other logical functions (e.g., OR) to create more complex conditional expressions.

Note: The AND function helps streamline data analysis by allowing you to evaluate whether multiple conditions are simultaneously met, which can be useful for data filtering, calculations, and more.

2.3 OR

Description:

The OR function in Tableau is a logical function used to combine multiple conditions and determine if at least one of them is true. It returns a Boolean result, which is true if any of the conditions are true, and false only if all conditions are false. The OR function is often used to create more complex conditional logic.

Syntax:

The syntax for the OR function is as follows:

```
OR(condition1, condition2, ...)
```

- `condition1`, `condition2`, etc.: These are the individual logical conditions you want to combine. You can include as many conditions as needed.

Example Usage:

Suppose you have a dataset of job applicants, and you want to identify applicants who either have a master's degree or more than five years of experience. You can use the OR function as follows:

```tableau
OR([Education] = 'Master's Degree', [Years of Experience] > 5)
```

- In this example, the OR function evaluates two conditions:

  - `[Education] = 'Master's Degree'`: Checks if the applicant has a master's degree.

- `[Years of Experience] > 5`: Checks if the applicant has more than five years of experience.

Explanation of the Code:

- The OR function combines the two conditions.

- If either of the conditions is true for a specific applicant, the function returns true; it returns false only if both conditions are false.

Tips:

1. The OR function is useful when you want to apply multiple criteria to filter or categorize data and need to identify records that meet any of the specified conditions.

2. Ensure that the individual conditions are structured correctly and evaluate the desired aspects of your data.

3. You can nest OR functions within other logical functions (e.g., AND) to create more complex conditional expressions.

Note: The OR function helps streamline data analysis by allowing you to evaluate whether at least one of multiple conditions is met, which can be useful for data filtering, categorization, and more.

2.4 NOT

Description:

The NOT function in Tableau is a logical function used to reverse the logical value of a condition or expression. It returns the opposite of the original condition. If the condition is true, NOT returns false, and if the condition is false, NOT returns true. NOT is often used to negate or reverse the outcome of a logical expression.

Syntax:

The syntax for the NOT function is as follows:

```
NOT(condition)
```

- `condition`: This is the logical condition or expression you want to reverse. It can be any valid condition or expression.

Example Usage:

Suppose you have a dataset of product prices, and you want to identify products that are not on sale (i.e., their 'On Sale' field is false). You can use the NOT function as follows:

```tableau
NOT([On Sale] = TRUE)
```

- In this example, the NOT function takes the condition `[On Sale] = TRUE`.

- It returns false for products that are on sale (where `[On Sale]` is true) and true for products that are not on sale (where `[On Sale]` is false).

Explanation of the Code:

- The NOT function reverses the logical value of the condition.

- If the condition is true (product is on sale), NOT returns false; if the condition is false (product is not on sale), NOT returns true.

Tips:

1. The NOT function is helpful for inverting logical conditions and making them more flexible in data analysis and visualization.

2. Ensure that the condition you provide is structured correctly to achieve the desired reversal.

3. You can use the NOT function in combination with other logical functions (e.g., AND, OR) to create more complex conditional expressions.

Note: The NOT function allows you to reverse the outcome of a logical condition, which can be valuable for situations where you want to identify records that do not meet a specific criterion.

2.5 XOR

Description:

The XOR function in Tableau is a logical function used to evaluate whether an odd number of conditions or expressions are true. XOR stands for "exclusive or," and it returns true if an odd number of conditions are true and false otherwise. XOR is used to create conditional logic that requires an exclusive combination of true conditions.

Syntax:

The syntax for the XOR function is as follows:

```
```

XOR(condition1, condition2, ...)

```
```

- `condition1`, `condition2`, etc.: These are the individual logical conditions or expressions you want to evaluate. You can include as many conditions as needed.

Example Usage:

Suppose you have a dataset of job applicants, and you want to identify applicants who either have both a master's degree and more than five years of experience or have neither of these qualifications. You can use the XOR function as follows:

```tableau
XOR(

    [Education] = 'Master's Degree',

    [Years of Experience] > 5

)
```

- In this example, the XOR function evaluates two conditions:

  - `[Education] = 'Master's Degree'`: Checks if the applicant has a master's degree.

  - `[Years of Experience] > 5`: Checks if the applicant has more than five years of experience.

Explanation of the Code:

- The XOR function evaluates whether an odd number of conditions are true.

- If either the first condition or the second condition is true but not both, XOR returns true; otherwise, it returns false.

Tips:

1. XOR is useful when you need to ensure an exclusive combination of true conditions, meaning that only one of the conditions is true but not both.

2. Ensure that the individual conditions are structured correctly and evaluate the desired aspects of your data.

3. XOR can be employed with more than two conditions when necessary.

Note: The XOR function allows you to create exclusive conditional logic in situations where you want to identify records that meet specific criteria exclusively, meaning they meet one condition but not both.

2.6 IIF

Description:

The IIF function in Tableau is a conditional function used to perform IF-THEN-ELSE logic in calculations. It allows you to evaluate a condition and return one value if the condition is true and another value if the condition is false. IIF is commonly used to create calculated fields that depend on specific conditions.

Syntax:

The syntax for the IIF function is as follows:

```
IIF(condition, value_if_true, value_if_false)
```

- `condition`: This is the logical condition you want to evaluate. If the condition is true, the function returns `value_if_true`; otherwise, it returns `value_if_false`.

- `value_if_true`: The value to be returned if the `condition` is true.

- `value_if_false`: The value to be returned if the `condition` is false.

Example Usage:

Suppose you have a dataset of product prices, and you want to create a calculated field that categorizes products as "Expensive" if the price is greater than $100 and "Affordable" if the price is $100 or less. You can use the IIF function as follows:

```tableau
IIF([Price] > 100, "Expensive", "Affordable")
```

- In this example, the `condition` `[Price] > 100` is evaluated for each product's price.

- If the condition is true (the price is greater than $100), the function returns "Expensive"; otherwise, it returns "Affordable."

Explanation of the Code:

- The IIF function evaluates the `condition` for each product.

- If the `condition` is true, "Expensive" is returned; otherwise, "Affordable" is returned.

Tips:

1. IIF is a versatile function for creating calculated fields that depend on specific conditions or criteria.

2. Ensure that the `condition`, `value_if_true`, and `value_if_false` are appropriate for the specific context of your data analysis.

3. You can nest IIF functions to handle multiple conditions and outcomes, creating more complex logic.

Note: The IIF function is a fundamental tool for applying IF-THEN-ELSE logic in Tableau calculations, allowing you to tailor your analysis and visualizations to specific conditions and scenarios.

2.7 IMPLIES

Description:

The IMPLIES function in Tableau is a logical function used to evaluate whether one condition implies another. It checks if a specific condition is true, and if it is, it returns the value associated with the implication; otherwise, it returns a different value. IMPLIES is commonly used in conditional logic to determine if a certain condition leads to a particular outcome.

Syntax:

The syntax for the IMPLIES function is as follows:

```
IMPLIES(condition, value_if_true, value_if_false)
```

- `condition`: This is the logical condition you want to evaluate. If the condition is true, the function returns `value_if_true`; otherwise, it returns `value_if_false`.

- `value_if_true`: The value to be returned if the `condition` is true and the implication holds.

- `value_if_false`: The value to be returned if the `condition` is true but the implication does not hold.

Example Usage:

Suppose you have a dataset of product prices and want to create a calculated field to determine if a product is "Premium" if the price is greater than $500, but only if the product is in stock. You can use the IMPLIES function as follows:

```tableau
IMPLIES([Price] > 500, IF [In Stock] = TRUE THEN "Premium" ELSE "Standard" END, "Standard")
```

- In this example, the `condition` `[Price] > 500` is evaluated to check if the price is greater than $500.

- If this condition is true, the IMPLIES function further evaluates the condition `[In Stock] = TRUE`. If it is true, "Premium" is returned; otherwise, "Standard" is returned.

Explanation of the Code:

- The IMPLIES function checks if the price is greater than $500.

- If the price is greater than $500, it checks if the product is in stock.

- If both conditions are true, "Premium" is returned; if not, "Standard" is returned.

Tips:

1. IMPLIES is useful for creating conditional logic based on the implication of one condition by another.

2. Ensure that the `condition`, `value_if_true`, and `value_if_false` are appropriate for your specific context of data analysis.

3. You can nest IMPLIES functions to handle multiple conditions and implications, creating more complex logic.

Note: The IMPLIES function is a valuable tool for applying conditional logic based on the implication of one condition by another, allowing you to create tailored calculations and visualizations.

III.
Date Time Functions

3.1 DATEADD

Description:

The DATEADD function in Tableau is used for date calculations and is used to add a specified interval of time to a given date. It allows you to perform operations like adding days, months, years, or other time units to a date, making it useful for date-related calculations and analysis.

Syntax:

The syntax for the DATEADD function is as follows:

```
DATEADD(interval, number, date)
```

- `interval`: This is the time unit that you want to add (e.g., 'day', 'month', 'year').

- `number`: The number of intervals you want to add to the date.

- `date`: The starting date to which you want to add the intervals.

Example Usage:

Suppose you have a dataset with order dates, and you want to create a calculated field that adds 7 days to each order date, predicting the delivery date. You can use the DATEADD function as follows:

```tableau
DATEADD('day', 7, [Order Date])
```

- In this example, the `interval` is 'day', and you want to add 7 days to each order date `[Order Date]`.

Explanation of the Code:

- The DATEADD function adds 7 days to each order date.

- It calculates the delivery date, assuming orders take 7 days to be delivered.

Tips:

1. The DATEADD function is versatile and can be used to perform various date-related calculations, such as projecting future dates or calculating the difference between two dates.

2. Ensure that the `interval` is chosen correctly based on the time unit you want to add.

3. Be mindful of how adding intervals may affect dates, considering factors like leap years and month lengths.

Note: The DATEADD function is a valuable tool for performing date calculations in Tableau, allowing you to manipulate dates for various analytical and reporting purposes.

3.2 DATEDIFF

Description:

The DATEDIFF function in Tableau is used for date calculations and is designed to calculate the difference between two dates in terms of a specified time unit (e.g., days, months, years). It enables you to measure the duration between two dates, which is valuable for analyzing time-based data.

Syntax:

The syntax for the DATEDIFF function is as follows:

```
DATEDIFF(interval, start_date, end_date)
```

- `interval`: This is the time unit in which you want to express the difference (e.g., 'day', 'month', 'year').

- `start_date`: The initial date from which the difference is calculated.

- `end_date`: The final date up to which the difference is calculated.

Example Usage:

Suppose you have a dataset with order dates and delivery dates, and you want to create a calculated field that calculates the number of days it took for each order to be delivered. You can use the DATEDIFF function as follows:

```tableau
DATEDIFF('day', [Order Date], [Delivery Date])
```

- In this example, the `interval` is 'day', and you want to calculate the number of days between `[Order Date]` and `[Delivery Date]`.

Explanation of the Code:

- The DATEDIFF function calculates the difference in days between the order date and delivery date.

- It provides the number of days it took for each order to be delivered.

Tips:

1. The DATEDIFF function is a useful tool for calculating date-based differences in your data, allowing you to analyze durations, response times, and more.

2. Choose the `interval` that aligns with the unit of time you want to measure.

3. Pay attention to the order of dates (e.g., start_date and end_date) as it affects the direction of the difference calculation.

Note: The DATEDIFF function is valuable for understanding the time-based relationships in your data and can be applied in various scenarios where you need to measure date-based durations.

3.3 DATEPARSE

Description:

The DATEPARSE function in Tableau is used to parse and convert a text string into a date or datetime format. It is particularly useful when you have date or time information stored as text and need to convert it into a date format that can be used for date calculations and analysis.

Syntax:

The syntax for the DATEPARSE function is as follows:

```
DATEPARSE(format, date_string)
```

- `format`: This is a string that defines the format of the date or datetime in the `date_string`. It specifies how the date information is represented in the text.

- `date_string`: The text string that contains the date or datetime information you want to parse and convert.

Example Usage:

Suppose you have a dataset with date information stored as text in the format "MM/dd/yyyy" (e.g., "10/15/2023"), and you want to convert it into a date format for analysis. You can use the DATEPARSE function as follows:

```tableau
DATEPARSE('MM/dd/yyyy', '10/15/2023')
```

- In this example, the `format` is 'MM/dd/yyyy', which matches the format of the date string '10/15/2023'.

Explanation of the Code:

- The DATEPARSE function takes the format 'MM/dd/yyyy' and parses the date string '10/15/2023'.

- It converts the text string into a date format that can be used for date calculations and analysis.

Tips:

1. DATEPARSE is essential when dealing with date or time data stored as text. It allows you to transform the data into a usable date format.

2. Ensure that the `format` parameter matches the actual format of the date string to avoid parsing errors.

3. Familiarize yourself with the date format codes (e.g., 'MM' for month, 'dd' for day, 'yyyy' for year) to specify the correct format.

Note: The DATEPARSE function is a powerful tool for converting text-based date information into a structured date format, enabling you to perform date calculations and analysis on your data.

3.4 DATESERIAL

Description:

The DATESERIAL function in Tableau is used to create a date or datetime value by specifying individual components such as year, month, and day. It is particularly useful when you have separate components of a date, and you want to combine them into a single date format for analysis or visualization.

Syntax:

The syntax for the DATESERIAL function is as follows:

```
DATESERIAL(year, month, day)
```

- `year`: This is the year component you want to use in the date.

- `month`: The month component you want to use (1-12).

- `day`: The day component you want to use (1-31).

Example Usage:

Suppose you have a dataset with separate columns for year, month, and day, and you want to create a single date field for analysis. You can use the DATESERIAL function as follows:

```tableau
DATESERIAL([Year], [Month], [Day])
```

- In this example, the function combines the values from the columns `[Year]`, `[Month]`, and `[Day]` to create a single date field.

Explanation of the Code:

- The DATESERIAL function takes the year, month, and day components and combines them into a single date value.

- This allows you to represent the date in a format that can be used for analysis or visualization.

Tips:

1. DATESERIAL is valuable when you have date components stored in separate fields and need to create a complete date for analysis.

2. Ensure that the components (year, month, day) are appropriate for the context of your data and follow the specified range and format.

3. Pay attention to the order of the components, as it may affect the date format (e.g., year, month, day).

Note: The DATESERIAL function is a practical tool for creating date fields in Tableau when your data is structured with separate date components, allowing you to work with complete date values in your analysis and visualizations.

3.5 DATESTR

Description:

The DATESTR function in Tableau is used to format a date or datetime value as a text string. It allows you to customize the presentation of dates in a human-readable format, making it useful for displaying dates in reports and visualizations.

Syntax:

The syntax for the DATESTR function is as follows:

```
DATESTR(format, date)
```

- `format`: This is a string that specifies the desired format for the date. It defines how the date should be represented as a text string.

- `date`: The date or datetime value that you want to format as a text string.

Example Usage:

Suppose you have a date field and want to display it in a more user-friendly format, such as "Month DD, YYYY" (e.g., "October 15, 2023"). You can use the DATESTR function as follows:

```tableau
DATESTR('MMMM dd, yyyy', [Order Date])
```

- In this example, the `format` is 'MMMM dd, yyyy', and you want to format the `[Order Date]` as a text string in this format.

Explanation of the Code:

- The DATESTR function takes the date value from `[Order Date]` and formats it as a text string in the specified format.

- It allows you to customize the way the date is presented for reporting and visualization.

Tips:

1. DATESTR is useful when you want to control how dates are displayed in your reports and visualizations, tailoring the format to your audience's needs.

2. Choose the `format` carefully to ensure that the resulting date text string meets your desired presentation.

3. Familiarize yourself with the date format codes (e.g., 'MMMM' for full month name, 'dd' for day, 'yyyy' for year) to specify the correct format.

Note: The DATESTR function is a valuable tool for formatting dates as text strings in Tableau, allowing you to create user-friendly date representations in your reports and visualizations.

3.6 DATETRUNC

Description:

The DATETRUNC function in Tableau is used for date calculations and is designed to truncate or round a date or datetime value to a specified level of precision. It allows you to focus on specific components of a date, such as years, quarters, or minutes, making it useful for summarizing and aggregating data at different time intervals.

Syntax:

The syntax for the DATETRUNC function is as follows:

```
DATETRUNC(level_of_precision, date)
```

- `level_of_precision`: This is a string that specifies the level of precision to which you want to truncate or round the date. It determines the resulting date's components (e.g., 'year', 'quarter', 'minute').

- `date`: The date or datetime value that you want to truncate or round.

Example Usage:

Suppose you have a dataset with order dates, and you want to create a calculated field that truncates the dates to the nearest quarter, allowing you to analyze quarterly trends. You can use the DATETRUNC function as follows:

```tableau
DATETRUNC('quarter', [Order Date])
```

- In this example, the `level_of_precision` is 'quarter', and you want to truncate the `[Order Date]` to the nearest quarter.

Explanation of the Code:

- The DATETRUNC function takes the `[Order Date]` and truncates it to the nearest quarter.

- It allows you to focus on quarterly trends in your data by summarizing dates at the quarter level of precision.

Tips:

1. DATETRUNC is valuable when you need to aggregate and summarize data based on specific time intervals or components of dates.

2. Choose the appropriate `level_of_precision` to align with the time intervals relevant to your analysis.

3. Understand that the choice of `level_of_precision` affects how the date components are truncated or rounded.

Note: The DATETRUNC function is a versatile tool for aggregating and summarizing data at different time intervals, allowing you to gain insights into trends and patterns in your time-based data.

Description:

The NOW function in Tableau is used to obtain the current date and time at the moment when the calculation or visualization is performed. It provides a dynamic timestamp and is often used for real-time or time-sensitive analysis and reporting.

Syntax:

The NOW function does not require any additional parameters, and its syntax is as follows:

```
NOW()
```

Example Usage:

Suppose you want to create a calculated field that captures the current date and time whenever a visualization is viewed or a report is generated. You can use the NOW function as follows:

```tableau
NOW()
```

- In this example, the NOW function is used without any parameters, returning the current date and time at the moment of calculation.

Explanation of the Code:

- The NOW function generates a dynamic timestamp representing the current date and time when the calculation is performed.

- It provides real-time information that can be used for various purposes, such as tracking when a report was viewed or analyzing data at the current moment.

Tips:

1. NOW is valuable for capturing real-time data or generating dynamic timestamps in your Tableau calculations and visualizations.

2. Be aware that the NOW function will provide a different timestamp every time it is recalculated, reflecting the current moment.

3. Use NOW in scenarios where you need to track or analyze data based on the current date and time.

Note: The NOW function is a useful tool for incorporating real-time or time-sensitive information into your Tableau work, enabling you to create dynamic and up-to-date reports and analyses.

3.8 DATEPART

Description:

The DATEPART function in Tableau is used to extract specific components or attributes from a date or datetime value. It allows you to focus on particular parts of a date, such as the year, quarter, month, day, hour, minute, and more. DATEPART is useful for various date-based calculations and visualizations.

Syntax:

The syntax for the DATEPART function is as follows:

```
DATEPART('datepart', date)
```

- `'datepart'`: This is a string that specifies the date component you want to extract (e.g., 'year', 'quarter', 'month', 'day', 'hour', 'minute').

- `date`: The date or datetime value from which you want to extract the specified component.

Example Usage:

Suppose you have a dataset with order dates, and you want to create a calculated field that extracts the month from each order date. You can use the DATEPART function as follows:

```tableau
DATEPART('month', [Order Date])
```

- In this example, the `'datepart'` is 'month', and you want to extract the month component from the `[Order Date]`.

Explanation of the Code:

- The DATEPART function extracts the month component from each `[Order Date]`.

- It provides a numerical representation of the month for each date in the dataset.

Tips:

1. DATEPART is valuable when you need to analyze or visualize data based on specific date components.

2. Choose the appropriate `'datepart'` to align with the aspect of the date you want to extract (e.g., 'month' for months).

3. Understand that DATEPART returns the numerical value of the specified date component.

Note: The DATEPART function is a versatile tool for extracting date components from date values, allowing you to perform various date-based calculations and create insightful visualizations based on specific date attributes.

3.9 DATEVALUE

Description:

The DATEVALUE function in Tableau is used to convert a date or datetime text string into a date value. It's particularly valuable when you have date information stored as text and need to transform it into a format that can be used for date calculations, comparisons, and analysis.

Syntax:

The syntax for the DATEVALUE function is as follows:

```
DATEVALUE(date_string)
```

- `date_string`: This is the text string containing the date or datetime information you want to convert into a date value.

Example Usage:

Suppose you have a dataset with date information stored as text in the format "yyyy-MM-dd" (e.g., "2023-10-15"), and you want to convert it into a date format for analysis. You can use the DATEVALUE function as follows:

```tableau
DATEVALUE('2023-10-15')
```

- In this example, the `date_string` is '2023-10-15', and you want to convert it into a date value.

Explanation of the Code:

- The DATEVALUE function takes the text string '2023-10-15' and converts it into a date value that can be used for date calculations, comparisons, and analysis.

Tips:

1. DATEVALUE is essential when working with date or time data stored as text. It allows you to convert text-based date information into a structured date format.

2. Ensure that the `date_string` is in a format that Tableau can recognize to avoid conversion errors.

3. After converting to a date value, you can perform various date-based operations, such as date arithmetic and comparisons.

Note: The DATEVALUE function is a practical tool for transforming date information stored as text into a structured date format, enabling you to work with dates effectively in your Tableau analysis and visualizations.

3.10 TODAY

Description:

The `TODAY` function in Tableau is a simple yet valuable date function that allows you to retrieve the current date. This function is widely used for various date-related calculations and comparisons in your Tableau worksheets and dashboards. It can be beneficial for tracking data freshness, filtering data by today's date, or creating dynamic date calculations.

Syntax:

```
TODAY()
```

Example:

Suppose you are working with a sales dataset, and you want to create a calculated field that identifies all the orders placed today. You can use the `TODAY` function for this purpose.

1. First, create a calculated field by right-clicking in the Data pane and selecting "Create Calculated Field."

2. Name the calculated field (e.g., "Orders Today").

3. Enter the following formula:

```tableau
IF [Order Date] = TODAY() THEN "Placed Today" ELSE "Not Placed Today" END
```

Explanation of the Example:

- The `IF` statement checks if the "Order Date" in your dataset is equal to the result of the `TODAY()` function. If a date matches the current date, it returns "Placed Today"; otherwise, it returns "Not Placed Today."

- This calculated field can be used in your visualization to filter or categorize orders based on whether they were placed on the current date or not.

Tips:

1. The `TODAY` function automatically takes the system date from your computer, so it provides the current date when you refresh your Tableau workbook.

2. You can also use the `TODAY` function in combination with other date functions, such as `DATEDIFF` or `DATEADD`, to perform more complex date calculations, like finding the number of days between two dates or calculating future dates.

3.11 DATENAME

Description:

The `DATENAME` function in Tableau is used to extract and return a specific component or part of a date, such as the year, quarter, month, day, or day of the week, from a given date field. This function is handy for breaking down date values into their individual components, allowing for detailed analysis and visualization of data over time.

Syntax:

```
DATENAME(date_part, date_expression)
```

- `date_part`: This is a string or keyword that specifies the part of the date you want to extract (e.g., "year," "quarter," "month," "day," "weekday").

- `date_expression`: The date field or calculation containing the date you want to extract from.

Example:

Let's say you have a dataset containing sales transactions with a "Order Date" field. You want to create a calculated field to extract the month and day of the week for each transaction.

1. Create a calculated field named "Order Month" for extracting the month:

```tableau
DATENAME('month', [Order Date])
```

2. Create another calculated field named "Order Day of the Week" for extracting the day of the week:

```tableau
DATENAME('weekday', [Order Date])
```

Explanation of the Example:

- In the first calculated field, we use the `DATENAME` function to extract the month component from the "Order Date" field. It returns the month name as a string (e.g., "January," "February").

- In the second calculated field, we use the `DATENAME` function to extract the day of the week from the "Order Date" field. It returns the day of the week name as a string (e.g., "Sunday," "Monday").

- These calculated fields can be used for visualizations, filtering, and grouping data based on the extracted date components.

Tips:

1. The `date_part` parameter should be enclosed in single quotes (' ') and must be a valid date component (e.g., 'year,' 'quarter,' 'month,' 'day,' 'weekday'). Using incorrect values may lead to errors.

2. You can use the `DATENAME` function with various date fields, and it's especially helpful when you need to present date-related information in a user-friendly format in your Tableau visualizations.

3. Ensure that the date format and data type of your date field are correctly set in Tableau to avoid unexpected results when using the `DATENAME` function.

3.12 MAKEDATE

Description:

The `MAKEDATE` function in Tableau is used to create a date from specified year, month, and day values. This function is particularly useful when you need to generate custom date values for various calculations, visualizations, or filtering data based on specific date criteria.

Syntax:

```
MAKEDATE(year, month, day)
```

- `year`: An integer representing the year for the date.

- `month`: An integer representing the month (1 for January, 2 for February, etc.).

- `day`: An integer representing the day of the month.

Example:

Suppose you want to create a calculated field that generates a custom date representing the 4th of July for a visualization.

1. Create a calculated field named "Custom 4th of July Date" using the `MAKEDATE` function:

```tableau
MAKEDATE(2023, 7, 4)
```

Explanation of the Example:

- In the calculated field, we use the `MAKEDATE` function to generate a custom date for the year 2023, in the 7th month (July), and on the 4th day of the month. The function returns a date value of July 4, 2023.

- This calculated field can be used in visualizations or filtering to display data related to the 4th of July.

Tips:

1. Ensure that the provided values for `year`, `month`, and `day` are valid and within the supported date range. Using incorrect values may result in errors or unexpected outcomes.

2. The `MAKEDATE` function is particularly useful when you need to create custom date values for various scenarios, such as holidays, specific events, or dynamic calculations.

3. When using this function, make sure the date format and data type settings for your calculated field are appropriately configured to match your visualization needs.

3.13 MAKEDATETIME

Description:

The `MAKEDATETIME` function in Tableau is used to create a date and time value from specified year, month, day, hour, minute, and second values. This function is helpful when you need to generate custom date and time values for various calculations, visualizations, or filtering data based on specific date and time criteria.

Syntax:

```
MAKEDATETIME(year, month, day, hour, minute, second)
```

- `year`: An integer representing the year for the date and time.

- `month`: An integer representing the month (1 for January, 2 for February, etc.).

- `day`: An integer representing the day of the month.

- `hour`: An integer representing the hour (24-hour format).

- `minute`: An integer representing the minute.

- `second`: An integer representing the second.

Example:

Suppose you want to create a calculated field that generates a custom date and time representing January 15, 2023, at 3:30:15 PM.

1. Create a calculated field named "Custom Date and Time" using the `MAKEDATETIME` function:

```tableau

MAKEDATETIME(2023, 1, 15, 15, 30, 15)

```

Explanation of the Example:

- In the calculated field, we use the `MAKEDATETIME` function to generate a custom date and time for the year 2023, in the 1st month (January), on the 15th day of the month, at 3:30:15 PM. The function returns a date and time value of January 15, 2023, at 3:30:15 PM.

- This calculated field can be used in visualizations, filtering, or for tracking events occurring at specific date and time values.

Tips:

1. Ensure that the provided values for `year`, `month`, `day`, `hour`, `minute`, and `second` are valid and within the supported date and time range. Using incorrect values may result in errors or unexpected outcomes.

2. The `MAKEDATETIME` function is particularly useful when you need to create custom date and time values for various scenarios, such as tracking events, scheduling, or dynamic calculations.

3. When using this function, make sure the date and time format and data type settings for your calculated field are appropriately configured to match your visualization needs.

3.14 MAKEPERIOD

Description:

The `MAKEPERIOD` function in Tableau is used to create a period data type representing a time period within the given parameters. This function is particularly useful when you need to define custom time intervals, such as fiscal quarters or other reporting periods, for data analysis, visualization, or calculations.

Syntax:

```

MAKEPERIOD(start_date, end_date, period_type)

```

- `start_date`: The start date of the period.

- `end_date`: The end date of the period.

- `period_type`: An optional parameter that specifies the type of period, such as "quarter" or "fiscal-year." If not provided, Tableau will determine the period type based on the provided dates.

Example:

Suppose you want to create a calculated field that represents the first quarter of the fiscal year 2023, which runs from October 1, 2022, to December 31, 2022.

1. Create a calculated field named "Fiscal Q1 2023" using the `MAKEPERIOD` function:

```tableau
MAKEPERIOD(#10/01/2022#, #12/31/2022#, "quarter")
```

Explanation of the Example:

- In the calculated field, we use the `MAKEPERIOD` function to define a custom period that represents the first quarter of the fiscal year 2023. The start date is October 1, 2022, and the end date is December 31, 2022. We also specify the period type as "quarter" to indicate that it's a quarterly period.

- The function returns a period object representing the first quarter of the fiscal year 2023, which can be used in calculations, filtering, and visualizations.

Tips:

1. Ensure that the `start_date` and `end_date` parameters are provided in the correct date format, typically using `#` delimiters, and are within a valid date range. Providing invalid dates may result in errors.

2. Periods created using the `MAKEPERIOD` function can be helpful for organizing and summarizing data based on custom time intervals, such as fiscal quarters or reporting periods.

3. Period objects created with this function can be used in calculations, filtering, and for defining custom date hierarchies for more flexible time-based analysis.

4. If the `period_type` parameter is omitted, Tableau will automatically determine the period type based on the provided dates, simplifying the process for creating periods.

IV.
String Functions

4.1 LEN

Description:

The LEN function in Tableau is used to determine the length (number of characters) of a given string. It provides a count of the characters in the string, including letters, digits, spaces, and any other characters.

Syntax:

The syntax for the LEN function is as follows:

```
LEN(string)
```

- `string`: This is the string for which you want to calculate the length.

Example Usage:

Suppose you have a dataset with product names, and you want to create a calculated field to find the length of each product name. You can use the LEN function as follows:

```tableau
LEN([Product Name])
```

- In this example, the `string` is `[Product Name]`, and you want to determine the length of each product name.

Explanation of the Code:

- The LEN function calculates the length of each product name in the dataset.

- It counts all the characters in the string, providing a numerical value for the length.

Tips:

1. LEN is useful when you need to determine the length of strings in your data, which can be valuable for various text-based calculations and analyses.

2. Ensure that the data type of the field or column you're using with LEN is a string or text field.

3. Keep in mind that the length is counted inclusively, so it includes all characters, including spaces and special characters.

Note: The LEN function is a practical tool for working with text data in Tableau, allowing you to calculate the length of strings and use this information in various calculations and visualizations.

Description:

The LEFT function in Tableau is used to extract a specified number of characters from the beginning (left side) of a given string. This function is particularly useful when you need to work with a portion of a text string, such as the first few characters of a field.

Syntax:

The syntax for the LEFT function is as follows:

```
```

LEFT(string, length)

```
```

- `string`: This is the string from which you want to extract characters from the left side.

- `length`: The number of characters you want to extract from the left side of the string.

Example Usage:

Suppose you have a dataset with a column containing product codes, and you want to create a calculated field to extract the first three characters (prefix) of each product code. You can use the LEFT function as follows:

```tableau
LEFT([Product Code], 3)
```

- In this example, the `string` is `[Product Code]`, and you want to extract the first three characters from each product code.

Explanation of the Code:

- The LEFT function extracts the first three characters from each product code in the dataset.

- It provides a substring that represents the prefix of the product code.

Tips:

1. LEFT is useful when you need to work with a specific portion of a text string, such as extracting prefixes, area codes, or identifiers.

2. Ensure that the `length` parameter is appropriate for the context and doesn't exceed the length of the string.

3. LEFT is versatile and can be used in various scenarios where you need to manipulate text data.

Note: The LEFT function is a practical tool for working with text data in Tableau, allowing you to extract substrings from the beginning of text strings for various text-based operations and visualizations.

4.3 RIGHT

Description:

The RIGHT function in Tableau is used to extract a specified number of characters from the end (right side) of a given string. It allows you to work with a portion of a text string, such as the last few characters, and is particularly useful when you need to manipulate and analyze text data.

Syntax:

The syntax for the RIGHT function is as follows:

```
RIGHT(string, length)
```

- `string`: This is the string from which you want to extract characters from the right side.

- `length`: The number of characters you want to extract from the right side of the string.

Example Usage:

Suppose you have a dataset with customer IDs, and you want to create a calculated field to extract the last four characters (suffix) of each customer ID. You can use the RIGHT function as follows:

```tableau
RIGHT([Customer ID], 4)
```

- In this example, the `string` is `[Customer ID]`, and you want to extract the last four characters from each customer ID.

Explanation of the Code:

- The RIGHT function extracts the last four characters from each customer ID in the dataset.

- It provides a substring that represents the suffix of the customer ID.

Tips:

1. RIGHT is valuable when you need to work with a specific portion of a text string from the end, such as extracting suffixes, file extensions, or codes.

2. Ensure that the `length` parameter is appropriate for the context and doesn't exceed the length of the string.

3. RIGHT can be used in various scenarios where you need to manipulate and analyze text data.

Note: The RIGHT function is a practical tool for working with text data in Tableau, allowing you to extract substrings from the end of text strings for various text-based operations and visualizations.

4.4 MID

Description:

The MID function in Tableau is used to extract a specified number of characters from a given string, starting from a specific position. It allows you to work with a substring within a text string, providing flexibility in text manipulation and analysis.

Syntax:

The syntax for the MID function is as follows:

```
MID(string, start, length)
```

- `string`: This is the string from which you want to extract characters.

- `start`: The position (index) within the string where extraction should begin.

- `length`: The number of characters to extract from the specified position.

Example Usage:

Suppose you have a dataset with product descriptions, and you want to create a calculated field that extracts a specific phrase from each description, starting from the 10th character and including the next 5 characters. You can use the MID function as follows:

```tableau
MID([Product Description], 10, 5)
```

- In this example, the `string` is `[Product Description]`, `start` is 10, and `length` is 5, indicating that you want to extract 5 characters starting from the 10th character.

Explanation of the Code:

- The MID function extracts a substring from each `[Product Description]`.

- It begins extraction from the 10th character and takes the next 5 characters, providing a portion of the product description.

Tips:

1. MID is useful when you need to extract a specific portion of a text string, such as extracting substrings or phrases from within a larger text.

2. Ensure that the `start` and `length` parameters are appropriate for the context and do not exceed the boundaries of the string.

3. MID is versatile and can be used for various text manipulation tasks, including extracting keywords, codes, or relevant text from descriptions.

Note: The MID function is a valuable tool for working with text data in Tableau, allowing you to extract and work with substrings from within text strings, enhancing your text-based analysis and visualizations.

4.5 UPPER

Description:

The UPPER function in Tableau is used to convert all characters in a given string to uppercase. It is valuable for standardizing text data and making it case-insensitive for various text-based operations and comparisons.

Syntax:

The syntax for the UPPER function is straightforward:

```
UPPER(string)
```

- `string`: This is the string you want to convert to uppercase.

Example Usage:

Suppose you have a dataset with product names, and you want to create a calculated field to ensure that all product names are displayed in uppercase for consistency. You can use the UPPER function as follows:

```tableau
UPPER([Product Name])
```

- In this example, the `string` is `[Product Name]`, and you want to convert the product names to uppercase.

Explanation of the Code:

- The UPPER function takes each `[Product Name]` and converts all characters to uppercase.

- It ensures that all product names are displayed consistently in uppercase, regardless of their original case.

Tips:

1. UPPER is useful when you want to standardize text data to a common case, making it easier to perform case-insensitive comparisons and analyses.

2. Keep in mind that UPPER does not change the original data but provides an uppercase version for presentation or calculations.

3. Use UPPER in scenarios where you need to compare text data without considering differences in letter case.

Note: The UPPER function is a simple yet essential tool for working with text data in Tableau, allowing you to standardize the case of text fields for consistency and facilitating case-insensitive operations and comparisons.

4.6 LOWER

Description:

The LOWER function in Tableau is used to convert all characters in a given string to lowercase. It is a valuable tool for standardizing text data to lowercase, making it case-insensitive for various text-based operations and comparisons.

Syntax:

The syntax for the LOWER function is simple:

```
LOWER(string)
```

- `string`: This is the string you want to convert to lowercase.

Example Usage:

Suppose you have a dataset with customer names, and you want to create a calculated field to ensure that all customer names are displayed in lowercase for consistency. You can use the LOWER function as follows:

```tableau
LOWER([Customer Name])
```

- In this example, the `string` is `[Customer Name]`, and you want to convert the customer names to lowercase.

Explanation of the Code:

- The LOWER function takes each `[Customer Name]` and converts all characters to lowercase.

- It ensures that all customer names are displayed consistently in lowercase, regardless of their original case.

Tips:

1. LOWER is useful when you want to standardize text data to lowercase, making it easier to perform case-insensitive comparisons and analyses.

2. Keep in mind that LOWER does not change the original data but provides a lowercase version for presentation or calculations.

3. Use LOWER in scenarios where you need to compare text data without considering differences in letter case.

Note: The LOWER function is a straightforward yet important tool for working with text data in Tableau, allowing you to standardize the case of text fields to lowercase for consistency and facilitating case-insensitive operations and comparisons.

4.7 TRIM

Description:

The TRIM function in Tableau is used to remove leading and trailing spaces (whitespace) from a given string. It is a useful function for cleaning and formatting text data, ensuring consistency in the spacing of text values.

Syntax:

The syntax for the TRIM function is straightforward:

```
TRIM(string)
```

- `string`: This is the string from which you want to remove leading and trailing spaces.

Example Usage:

Suppose you have a dataset with product descriptions, and you want to create a calculated field to remove any leading or trailing spaces from each description. You can use the TRIM function as follows:

```tableau
TRIM([Product Description])
```

- In this example, the `string` is `[Product Description]`, and you want to remove any leading and trailing spaces from the product descriptions.

Explanation of the Code:

- The TRIM function takes each `[Product Description]` and removes any leading and trailing spaces, ensuring that the text is clean and formatted correctly.

- It ensures that there are no unwanted spaces at the beginning or end of the text.

Tips:

1. TRIM is useful when you need to clean and format text data, especially when text values may have inconsistent spacing.

2. Keep in mind that TRIM only removes spaces from the beginning and end of a string, not spaces within the text.

3. Use TRIM to prepare text data for analysis, filtering, or visualizations where leading and trailing spaces should not affect the results.

Note: The TRIM function is a handy tool for cleaning and formatting text data in Tableau, ensuring that text values are free of unnecessary leading and trailing spaces, which can impact data quality and consistency.

4.8 REPLACE

Description:

The REPLACE function in Tableau is used to replace occurrences of a specified substring within a given string with another substring. It is a powerful tool for text manipulation, allowing you to make changes to text data based on specific patterns.

Syntax:

The syntax for the REPLACE function is as follows:

```
REPLACE(string, search, replacement)
```

- `string`: This is the string in which you want to replace occurrences of a specified substring.

- `search`: The substring you want to search for and replace.

- `replacement`: The substring with which you want to replace the found occurrences of `search`.

Example Usage:

Suppose you have a dataset with product names, and you want to create a calculated field to replace all instances of "Ltd" with "Limited" in the product names. You can use the REPLACE function as follows:

```tableau
REPLACE([Product Name], "Ltd", "Limited")
```

- In this example, the `string` is `[Product Name]`, and you want to replace all occurrences of "Ltd" with "Limited."

Explanation of the Code:

- The REPLACE function takes each `[Product Name]` and replaces all instances of "Ltd" with "Limited," ensuring that the product names are consistent.

Tips:

1. REPLACE is valuable when you need to perform mass text replacements or standardize text data.

2. It can be used to correct typographical errors, replace abbreviations, or make consistent changes to text values.

3. Ensure that `search` is a specific substring to avoid unintended replacements within larger words or phrases.

Note: The REPLACE function is a versatile tool for text manipulation in Tableau, allowing you to make systematic changes to text data, correct errors, or standardize text values across your dataset.

4.9 FIND

Description:

The FIND function in Tableau is used to determine the starting position of a specified substring within a given string. It helps you identify the location of a substring within a text field, which can be valuable for text manipulation and analysis.

Syntax:

The syntax for the FIND function is as follows:

```
FIND(substring, string)
```

- `substring`: This is the substring you want to find within the `string`.

- `string`: The string in which you want to search for the `substring`.

Example Usage:

Suppose you have a dataset with email addresses, and you want to create a calculated field to find the position of the "@" symbol within each email address. You can use the FIND function as follows:

```tableau
FIND("@", [Email Address])
```

- In this example, the `substring` is the "@" symbol, and the `string` is `[Email Address]`, and you want to find the position of the "@" symbol.

Explanation of the Code:

- The FIND function searches each `[Email Address]` for the "@" symbol.

- It returns the position (index) where the "@" symbol is located within the email address.

Tips:

1. FIND is useful for locating specific substrings or characters within text fields.

2. The result is a numeric value representing the position of the found substring within the string.

3. Be aware that FIND returns 0 if the substring is not found in the string. You can use this information to handle missing or unexpected data.

Note: The FIND function is a practical tool for text manipulation and analysis in Tableau, helping you identify the positions of specific substrings within text fields, which can be used for various text-based operations and calculations.

4.10 CONTAINS

Description:

The CONTAINS function in Tableau is used to check if a specified substring or pattern exists within a given string. It allows you to perform text-based checks to determine whether a string contains a particular sub-string or sequence of characters.

Syntax:

The syntax for the CONTAINS function is as follows:

```
CONTAINS(string, substring)
```

- `string`: This is the string in which you want to search for the `substring`.

- `substring`: The substring or pattern you want to check for within the `string`.

Example Usage:

Suppose you have a dataset with product descriptions, and you want to create a calculated field to check if each description contains the word "discount." You can use the CONTAINS function as follows:

```tableau
CONTAINS([Product Description], "discount")
```

- In this example, the `string` is `[Product Description]`, and you want to check if "discount" exists in each product description.

Explanation of the Code:

- The CONTAINS function checks each `[Product Description]` for the presence of the substring "discount."

- It returns a Boolean value (TRUE or FALSE) indicating whether the specified substring exists within the description.

Tips:

1. CONTAINS is useful for performing text-based checks to identify specific keywords or patterns within text fields.

2. The result is a Boolean value, which can be used for filtering, grouping, or conditional calculations based on text content.

3. You can use CONTAINS in combination with other logical functions to create complex text-based conditions.

Note: The CONTAINS function is a valuable tool for text-based checks and filtering in Tableau, allowing you to identify whether specific substrings or patterns are present within text data, which can be beneficial for various text analysis and data visualization tasks.

4.11 SPLIT

Description:

The SPLIT function in Tableau is used to divide a string into separate parts based on a specified delimiter. It is valuable for breaking down text data into segments, which can be particularly useful when dealing with data that contains structured information separated by a common character or pattern.

Syntax:

The syntax for the SPLIT function is as follows:

```
SPLIT(string, delimiter)
```

- `string`: This is the string you want to split into parts.

- `delimiter`: The delimiter or character used to identify where to split the string.

Example Usage:

Suppose you have a dataset with addresses, and you want to create a calculated field to extract the city name from the full address. You can use the SPLIT function as follows:

```tableau
SPLIT([Full Address], ',')[0]
```

- In this example, the `string` is `[Full Address]`, and you want to split the address based on the comma (",") and extract the first part (index 0), which is typically the city.

Explanation of the Code:

- The SPLIT function divides the `[Full Address]` into parts based on the comma (",") delimiter.

- The `[0]` index refers to the first part, which is often the city name in addresses.

Tips:

1. SPLIT is beneficial when you need to extract specific segments from text data that is structured using delimiters.

2. You can use different delimiters, such as commas, spaces, or other characters, to split the text based on your data's format.

3. Be cautious about the order of parts after splitting, as it can vary depending on your data's structure.

Note: The SPLIT function is a useful tool for breaking down text data into separate segments in Tableau, allowing you to extract specific information from structured text fields. This function is particularly handy for cleaning, analyzing, and visualizing data with complex text formats.

4.12 CONCATENATE

Description:

The CONCATENATE function in Tableau is used to combine multiple text values into a single string. It allows you to create new text fields by joining together various text elements, such as columns, constants, or calculated values.

Syntax:

The syntax for the CONCATENATE function is as follows:

```
CONCATENATE(expression1, expression2, ...)
```

- `expression1`, `expression2`, ...: These are the expressions or text values you want to concatenate into a single string.

Example Usage:

Suppose you have a dataset with first names and last names, and you want to create a calculated field to generate full names. You can use the CONCATENATE function as follows:

```tableau
CONCATENATE([First Name], " ", [Last Name])
```

- In this example, `expression1` is `[First Name]`, and `expression2` is a space character (for separating the first and last names), and `expression3` is `[Last Name]`.

Explanation of the Code:

- The CONCATENATE function combines the `[First Name]`, a space character, and the `[Last Name]` into a single string, creating full names.

Tips:

1. CONCATENATE is helpful when you need to create new text fields by merging existing text values.

2. You can use multiple expressions to concatenate different parts and add separators as needed.

3. Ensure that expressions are in the correct order to achieve the desired formatting of the concatenated string.

Note: The CONCATENATE function is a versatile tool for text manipulation in Tableau, allowing you to generate new text values by combining various text elements. It is especially useful for creating user-friendly labels, generating full names, or formatting text for visualizations.

4.13 STR

Description:

The STR function in Tableau is used to convert numeric or date values into strings. It is particularly useful when you need to format numeric values as text for better presentation, or when you want to customize the appearance of date values in your visualizations.

Syntax:

The syntax for the STR function is as follows:

```
STR(expression, format)
```

- `expression`: This is the numeric or date value you want to convert to a string.

- `format`: The format in which you want to display the resulting string. This is optional and can be used to customize the appearance of the string.

Example Usage:

Suppose you have a dataset with numeric values representing sales amounts, and you want to create a calculated field to display these values as strings with a currency symbol and two decimal places. You can use the STR function as follows:

```tableau
STR([Sales Amount], "$#,###.##")
```

- In this example, `expression` is `[Sales Amount]`, and `format` is "$#,###.##," which specifies the desired currency format.

Explanation of the Code:

- The STR function converts the numeric values from `[Sales Amount]` into strings, following the specified format.

- The format "$#,###.##" adds a dollar sign, thousands separators, and two decimal places.

Tips:

1. STR is useful when you want to customize the display of numeric or date values in your visualizations.

2. The `format` parameter allows you to control the appearance of the resulting string, which can include symbols, separators, and decimal places.

3. Be aware that the format should match the data type of the `expression`.

Note: The STR function in Tableau provides a powerful way to format numeric and date values as strings, allowing you to enhance the visual presentation of your data in dashboards and reports.

4.14 REPLICATE

Description:

The REPLICATE function in Tableau is used to repeat a specified character or string a certain number of times. This function is helpful when you need to create repeated patterns or duplicate characters to achieve a particular format or structure in your data.

Syntax:

The syntax for the REPLICATE function is as follows:

```
REPLICATE(string, count)
```

- `string`: This is the character or string you want to repeat.

- `count`: The number of times you want to repeat the specified `string`.

Example Usage:

Suppose you have a dataset with a product rating field, and you want to create a calculated field that displays a star rating based on the rating value. You can use the REPLICATE function as follows:

```tableau
REPLICATE("*", [Rating])
```

- In this example, `string` is the asterisk ("*"), and `count` is the `[Rating]` value.

Explanation of the Code:

- The REPLICATE function repeats the asterisk character "*" a number of times equal to the `[Rating]`.

- For example, if the rating is 3, the result will be "*-*-*," indicating a 3-star rating.

Tips:

1. REPLICATE is useful when you need to generate repeated characters or strings to format data or create visual elements like stars, dots, or other patterns.

2. The `count` parameter should be a positive integer to specify the number of repetitions.

3. You can use the result in calculated fields to enhance data visualization and presentation.

Note: The REPLICATE function is a valuable tool for creating repeated characters or strings in Tableau, allowing you to generate patterns, symbols, or visual elements based on the values in your data, which can improve data visualization and dashboard design.

4.15 CONCAT

Description:

The CONCAT function in Tableau is used to combine multiple strings or expressions into a single string. It is particularly useful when you want to concatenate various text values, including column names, constants, or calculated fields, to create a single string for display or analysis.

Syntax:

The syntax for the CONCAT function is as follows:

```
CONCAT(expression1, expression2, ...)
```

- `expression1`, `expression2`, ...: These are the expressions or text values you want to concatenate into a single string.

Example Usage:

Suppose you have a dataset with first names and last names, and you want to create a calculated field to generate full names. You can use the CONCAT function as follows:

```tableau
CONCAT([First Name], " ", [Last Name])
```

- In this example, `expression1` is `[First Name]`, `expression2` is a space character (for separating the first and last names), and `expression3` is `[Last Name]`.

Explanation of the Code:

- The CONCAT function combines the `[First Name]`, a space character, and the `[Last Name]` into a single string, creating full names.

Tips:

1. CONCAT is helpful when you need to create new text fields by merging existing text values.

2. You can use multiple expressions to concatenate different parts and add separators as needed.

3. Ensure that expressions are in the correct order to achieve the desired formatting of the concatenated string.

Note: The CONCAT function is a versatile tool for text manipulation in Tableau, allowing you to generate new text values by combining various text elements. It is especially useful for creating user-friendly labels, generating full names, or formatting text for visualizations.

V.
Window Functions

5.1 WINDOW_AVG

Description:

The WINDOW_AVG function in Tableau is used to calculate the moving average of a numeric field within a specified window or range of data points. Moving averages are commonly used in time series analysis to smooth out fluctuations in data and identify trends.

Syntax:

The syntax for the WINDOW_AVG function is as follows:

```
WINDOW_AVG([expression], [start], [end])
```

- `[expression]`: This is the numeric field or expression for which you want to calculate the moving average.

- `[start]`: This parameter defines the starting point of the window, indicating how many data points to go back in the dataset.

- `[end]`: This parameter defines the ending point of the window, indicating how many data points to go forward in the dataset.

Example Usage:

Suppose you have a dataset with daily sales data, and you want to create a calculated field that shows a 7-day moving average of sales to identify trends. You can use the WINDOW_AVG function as follows:

```tableau
WINDOW_AVG([Sales], -6, 0)
```

- In this example, `[Sales]` represents the numeric field you want to calculate the moving average for. The `[start]` parameter is -6, indicating that the window starts 6 data points (days) back, and the `[end]` parameter is 0, indicating the current data point.

Explanation of the Code:

- The WINDOW_AVG function calculates the average of the `[Sales]` field for the previous 7 days (including the current day), creating a 7-day moving average.

Tips:

1. Use the WINDOW_AVG function to analyze trends and reduce noise in time series data.

2. Adjust the `[start]` and `[end]` parameters to change the length of the moving average window.

3. Be cautious with missing data points or data gaps, as they can affect the moving average calculation.

Note: WINDOW_AVG is a valuable function for time series analysis in Tableau, allowing you to visualize and analyze trends in data by smoothing out short-term fluctuations. It's commonly used for forecasting and identifying patterns in datasets with time-based information.

5.2 WINDOW_SUM

Description:

The WINDOW_SUM function in Tableau is used to calculate the sum of a numeric field within a specified window or range of data points. It allows you to create a running total or cumulative sum of data within the specified window, which is useful for various calculations and visualizations.

Syntax:

The syntax for the WINDOW_SUM function is as follows:

```
WINDOW_SUM([expression], [start], [end])
```

- `[expression]`: This is the numeric field or expression for which you want to calculate the sum.

- `[start]`: This parameter defines the starting point of the window, indicating how many data points to go back in the dataset.

- `[end]`: This parameter defines the ending point of the window, indicating how many data points to go forward in the dataset.

Example Usage:

Suppose you have a dataset with daily sales data, and you want to create a calculated field that shows a running total of sales for the last 30 days. You can use the WINDOW_SUM function as follows:

```tableau
WINDOW_SUM([Sales], -29, 0)
```

```
```

- In this example, `[Sales]` represents the numeric field for which you want to calculate the running total. The `[start]` parameter is -29, indicating that the window starts 29 data points (days) back, and the `[end]` parameter is 0, indicating the current data point.

Explanation of the Code:

- The WINDOW_SUM function calculates the sum of the `[Sales]` field for the last 30 days (including the current day), creating a running total of sales.

Tips:

1. Use the WINDOW_SUM function to create running totals and cumulative sums of data, which can be valuable for visualizing trends and analyzing accumulative data.

2. Adjust the `[start]` and `[end]` parameters to change the length of the window for calculating the running sum.

3. Be cautious with missing data points or data gaps, as they can affect the running total calculation.

Note: WINDOW_SUM is a powerful function in Tableau for calculating running totals and cumulative sums, especially in scenarios where you want to track progress or cumulative values over time. It's commonly used in financial analysis, inventory management, and various other fields where accumulating data is important.

5.3 WINDOW_MAX

Description:

The WINDOW_MAX function in Tableau is used to calculate the maximum value of a numeric field within a specified window or range of data points. It allows you to find the maximum value within a sliding window of data, which can be useful for identifying peaks or maximum values in time series or other data.

Syntax:

The syntax for the WINDOW_MAX function is as follows:

```
```

WINDOW_MAX([expression], [start], [end])

```
```

- `[expression]`: This is the numeric field or expression for which you want to find the maximum value.

- `[start]`: This parameter defines the starting point of the window, indicating how many data points to go back in the dataset.

- `[end]`: This parameter defines the ending point of the window, indicating how many data points to go forward in the dataset.

Example Usage:

Suppose you have a dataset with daily stock prices, and you want to create a calculated field that shows the maximum price in the last 15 days. You can use the WINDOW_MAX function as follows:

```tableau
```

WINDOW_MAX([Stock Price], -14, 0)

```
```

- In this example, `[Stock Price]` represents the numeric field for which you want to find the maximum value. The `[start]` parameter is -14, indicating that the window starts 14 data points (days) back, and the `[end]` parameter is 0, indicating the current data point.

Explanation of the Code:

- The WINDOW_MAX function calculates the maximum value of the `[Stock Price]` field within the last 15 days (including the current day).

Tips:

1. Use the WINDOW_MAX function to identify peaks or maximum values in a rolling or sliding window of data.

2. Adjust the `[start]` and `[end]` parameters to change the length of the window for finding the maximum value.

3. Be mindful of the window size and data frequency; a larger window may capture longer-term trends, while a smaller window may capture shorter-term fluctuations.

Note: WINDOW_MAX is a useful function for identifying maximum values within a specified window of data. It is commonly used in financial analysis, signal processing, and other fields where identifying peaks or extremes in a dataset is important.

5.4 WINDOW_MIN

Description:

The WINDOW_MIN function in Tableau is used to calculate the minimum value of a numeric field within a specified window or range of data points. It allows you to find the minimum value within a sliding window of data, which can be useful for identifying troughs or minimum values in time series or other data.

Syntax:

The syntax for the WINDOW_MIN function is as follows:

```
WINDOW_MIN([expression], [start], [end])
```

- `[expression]`: This is the numeric field or expression for which you want to find the minimum value.

- `[start]`: This parameter defines the starting point of the window, indicating how many data points to go back in the dataset.

- `[end]`: This parameter defines the ending point of the window, indicating how many data points to go forward in the dataset.

Example Usage:

Suppose you have a dataset with daily temperature data, and you want to create a calculated field that shows the minimum temperature in the last 7 days. You can use the WINDOW_MIN function as follows:

```tableau
```

```
WINDOW_MIN([Temperature], -6, 0)
```

- In this example, `[Temperature]` represents the numeric field for which you want to find the minimum value. The `[start]` parameter is -6, indicating that the window starts 6 data points (days) back, and the `[end]` parameter is 0, indicating the current data point.

Explanation of the Code:

- The WINDOW_MIN function calculates the minimum temperature in the last 7 days (including the current day), helping identify the coldest temperature during that period.

Tips:

1. Use the WINDOW_MIN function to identify troughs or minimum values in a rolling or sliding window of data.

2. Adjust the `[start]` and `[end]` parameters to change the length of the window for finding the minimum value.

3. Consider the context and data frequency; a larger window captures longer-term trends, while a smaller window captures shorter-term fluctuations.

Note: WINDOW_MIN is a useful function for identifying minimum values within a specified window of data. It is commonly used in meteorology, financial analysis, and various fields where identifying troughs or minimum points in a dataset is important.

5.5 WINDOW_COUNT

Description:

The WINDOW_COUNT function in Tableau is used to calculate the count of rows or data points within a specified window or range. It provides a count of how many data points are within a sliding window, making it useful for various analytical tasks, such as calculating moving averages or identifying patterns based on the number of data points in a window.

Syntax:

The syntax for the WINDOW_COUNT function is as follows:

```
```

```
WINDOW_COUNT([expression], [start], [end])
```

```
```

- `[expression]`: This can be any field or expression for which you want to count the data points.

- `[start]`: This parameter defines the starting point of the window, indicating how many data points to go back in the dataset.

- `[end]`: This parameter defines the ending point of the window, indicating how many data points to go forward in the dataset.

Example Usage:

Suppose you have a dataset with daily website traffic, and you want to create a calculated field that counts how many days had above-average traffic in the past 14 days. You can use the WINDOW_COUNT function as follows:

```tableau
```

```
WINDOW_COUNT(IF [Daily Traffic] > WINDOW_AVG([Daily Traffic], -13, 0) THEN 1
ELSE 0 END, -13, 0)
```

```

- In this example, `[Daily Traffic]` is the field you want to count data points for. The function counts the number of days when the daily traffic was greater than the average of the past 14 days.

**Explanation of the Code:**

- The WINDOW_COUNT function evaluates the condition for each day within the 14-day window (including the current day) and counts the days that meet the condition, i.e., have above-average traffic.

**Tips:**

1. Use WINDOW_COUNT to count data points within a specified window for various analytical tasks.

2. You can pair WINDOW_COUNT with other functions to calculate statistics, identify patterns, or create custom metrics based on the count of data points.

3. Adjust the `[start]` and `[end]` parameters to define the length of the window for counting data points as needed.

**Note:** WINDOW_COUNT is a versatile function that can be used in combination with other Tableau functions to gain insights from data by considering the number of data points within a defined window. It is valuable for time series analysis and various forms of data aggregation.
```

5.6 WINDOW_FIRST

Description:

The WINDOW_FIRST function in Tableau is used to retrieve the first value of an expression or field within a specified window or range of data points. It allows you to access the value of a field at the beginning of a sliding window, which can be valuable for various analytical tasks where the initial data point is important.

Syntax:

The syntax for the WINDOW_FIRST function is as follows:

```
```

WINDOW_FIRST([expression], [start], [end])

```
```

- `[expression]`: This can be any field or expression for which you want to retrieve the first value.

- `[start]`: This parameter defines the starting point of the window, indicating how many data points to go back in the dataset.

- `[end]`: This parameter defines the ending point of the window, indicating how many data points to go forward in the dataset.

Example Usage:

Suppose you have a dataset with daily stock prices, and you want to create a calculated field that shows the price of a stock at the beginning of the month. You can use the WINDOW_FIRST function as follows:

```tableau
WINDOW_FIRST([Stock Price], 0, 0)
```

```
```

- In this example, `[Stock Price]` is the field for which you want to retrieve the first value. The `[start]` and `[end]` parameters are both 0, indicating that you want the value of the current data point.

Explanation of the Code:

- The WINDOW_FIRST function provides the stock price at the beginning of the current month, helping you track the initial price for analytical purposes.

Tips:

1. Use WINDOW_FIRST to access the first value of an expression or field within a specified window.

2. This function is particularly useful for time-based data, such as tracking the opening price of a stock at the beginning of a month or the first customer interaction in a session.

3. Adjust the `[start]` and `[end]` parameters to define the length of the window as needed. In this example, both parameters are set to 0, indicating that you're looking at the current data point.

Note: WINDOW_FIRST is valuable for various scenarios where knowing the initial value within a window of data is critical for analysis or reporting. It is frequently used in finance, sales, and time series analysis.

5.7 WINDOW_LAST

Description:

The WINDOW_LAST function in Tableau is used to retrieve the last value of an expression or field within a specified window or range of data points. It allows you to access the value of a field at the end of a sliding window, which can be valuable for various analytical tasks where the final data point is important.

Syntax:

The syntax for the WINDOW_LAST function is as follows:

```
WINDOW_LAST([expression], [start], [end])
```

- `[expression]`: This can be any field or expression for which you want to retrieve the last value.

- `[start]`: This parameter defines the starting point of the window, indicating how many data points to go back in the dataset.

- `[end]`: This parameter defines the ending point of the window, indicating how many data points to go forward in the dataset.

Example Usage:

Suppose you have a dataset with daily sales data, and you want to create a calculated field that shows the total sales at the end of each month. You can use the WINDOW_LAST function as follows:

```tableau
WINDOW_LAST(SUM([Sales]), 0, 0)
```

```
```

- In this example, `SUM([Sales])` calculates the total sales, and you use the WINDOW_LAST function to retrieve the total sales for the current data point.

Explanation of the Code:

- The WINDOW_LAST function provides the total sales at the end of the current month, helping you track the final value for analytical purposes.

Tips:

1. Use WINDOW_LAST to access the last value of an expression or field within a specified window.

2. This function is particularly useful for time-based data, such as calculating the closing balance at the end of a financial period or tracking the total sales at the end of a month.

3. Adjust the `[start]` and `[end]` parameters to define the length of the window as needed. In this example, both parameters are set to 0, indicating that you're looking at the current data point.

Note: WINDOW_LAST is valuable for various scenarios where knowing the final value within a window of data is critical for analysis or reporting. It is frequently used in finance, sales, and time series analysis.

5.8 RANK

Description:

The RANK function in Tableau is used to assign a unique rank to each row or data point based on the values of a specified field. It is often used to identify the relative position of data points in a dataset and determine their ranking order.

Syntax:

The syntax for the RANK function is as follows:

```
```

RANK([expression], [order], [ties])

```
```

- `[expression]`: This is the field or expression for which you want to calculate the rank.

- `[order]`: It specifies the order in which the ranks should be assigned, either "asc" for ascending or "desc" for descending.

- `[ties]`: This parameter handles tied values and can be set to "min", "max", or "dense". "min" assigns the lowest rank to tied values, "max" assigns the highest rank, and "dense" assigns consecutive ranks to tied values.

Example Usage:

Suppose you have a dataset of student scores and you want to rank them based on their scores in descending order:

```tableau
RANK([Score], "desc", "min")
```

- In this example, the `RANK` function is used to assign ranks to students based on their scores in descending order, and in the case of tied scores, it assigns the lowest rank.

Explanation of the Code:

- The RANK function will provide a unique rank for each student based on their scores, with the highest score receiving the rank of 1.

Tips:

1. RANK is useful for determining the relative position or order of data points within a dataset.

2. The `[order]` parameter allows you to specify whether ranks should be assigned in ascending or descending order.

3. The `[ties]` parameter is helpful when dealing with tied values. Choose "min" for the lowest rank, "max" for the highest rank, or "dense" for consecutive ranks.

4. RANK is often used for creating leaderboards, ranking sales performance, or identifying the top and bottom performers in a dataset.

5.9 LAG

Description:

The LAG function in Tableau is used to access the value of a field from the previous row within a specified window or partition. It allows you to retrieve data from a previous row and incorporate it into your current row's calculations or analysis.

Syntax:

The syntax for the LAG function is as follows:

```
```

LAG(expression, [offset], [default])

```
```

- `expression`: The field or expression for which you want to retrieve the previous value.

- `offset`: It specifies the number of rows to go back to fetch the value. The default is 1, which refers to the immediately preceding row.

- `default`: This is an optional parameter and specifies the value to return if there is no previous row available. If not specified, it defaults to NULL.

Example Usage:

Suppose you have a dataset of daily stock prices, and you want to calculate the daily percentage change in stock price compared to the previous day:

```tableau

([Closing Price] - LAG([Closing Price])) / LAG([Closing Price])

```

- In this example, the expression calculates the percentage change in stock price by subtracting the previous day's closing price from the current day's closing price and then dividing by the previous day's closing price.

Explanation of the Code:

- The LAG function is used to retrieve the previous day's closing price and subtract it from the current day's closing price. The result is then divided by the previous day's closing price to calculate the percentage change.

Tips:

1. LAG is useful for performing calculations that involve the comparison of values with previous rows.

2. The `offset` parameter allows you to specify how many rows back to look for the previous value. By default, it looks at the immediately preceding row.

3. It's important to handle cases where there is no previous row available, which can be achieved by using the `default` parameter.

5.10 LEAD

Description:

The LEAD function in Tableau allows you to access the value of a field from the following row within a specified window or partition. It is the opposite of the LAG function, which retrieves values from previous rows. LEAD is useful for comparing data with future rows.

Syntax:

The syntax for the LEAD function is as follows:

```
```

```
LEAD(expression, [offset], [default])
```

```
```

- `expression`: The field or expression for which you want to retrieve the next (following) value.

- `offset`: It specifies the number of rows to move forward to fetch the value. The default is 1, which refers to the immediately following row.

- `default`: This is an optional parameter and specifies the value to return if there is no next row available. If not specified, it defaults to NULL.

Example Usage:

Suppose you have a dataset of daily stock prices, and you want to calculate the daily percentage change in stock price compared to the next day:

```tableau
([Closing Price] - LEAD([Closing Price])) / LEAD([Closing Price])
```

- In this example, the expression calculates the percentage change in stock price by subtracting the next day's closing price from the current day's closing price and then dividing by the next day's closing price.

Explanation of the Code:

- The LEAD function is used to retrieve the next day's closing price and subtract it from the current day's closing price. The result is then divided by the next day's closing price to calculate the percentage change.

Tips:

1. LEAD is useful for performing calculations that involve the comparison of values with future rows.

2. The `offset` parameter allows you to specify how many rows forward to look for the next value. By default, it looks at the immediately following row.

3. It's important to handle cases where there is no next row available, which can be achieved by using the `default` parameter.

VI.
Type Conversion Functions

6.1 TOINT

Description:

The TOINT function in Tableau is used for type conversion, specifically for converting a field or expression to an integer data type. This function is valuable when you need to change the data type of a field from another type, such as string or float, to an integer.

Syntax:

The syntax for the TOINT function is straightforward:

```
TOINT(expression)
```

- `expression`: This is the field or expression that you want to convert to an integer.

Example Usage:

Suppose you have a dataset with a field named "Age" stored as strings, and you want to convert it to integers:

```tableau
TOINT([Age])
```

Explanation of the Code:

- In this example, the TOINT function is applied to the "Age" field. It takes the values in the "Age" field, which are originally stored as strings, and converts them into integer data type. The result is a field with integer values.

Tips:

1. Use TOINT when you need to change the data type of a field to an integer.

2. Ensure that the values in the field you're converting can be validly represented as integers. If there are non-numeric characters, the conversion may result in null values or errors.

6.2 TOFLOAT

Description:

The TOFLOAT function in Tableau is used for type conversion, specifically for converting a field or expression to a floating-point number data type. This function is valuable when you need to change the data type of a field from another type, such as string or integer, to a float.

Syntax:

The syntax for the TOFLOAT function is straightforward:

```
```

TOFLOAT(expression)

```
```

- `expression`: This is the field or expression that you want to convert to a floating-point number.

Example Usage:

Suppose you have a dataset with a field named "Price" stored as strings, and you want to convert it to floating-point numbers:

```tableau
TOFLOAT([Price])
```

Explanation of the Code:

- In this example, the TOFLOAT function is applied to the "Price" field. It takes the values in the "Price" field, which are originally stored as strings, and converts them into floating-point numbers. The result is a field with decimal values.

Tips:

1. Use TOFLOAT when you need to change the data type of a field to a floating-point number.

2. Ensure that the values in the field you're converting can be validly represented as floating-point numbers. If there are non-numeric characters, the conversion may result in null values or errors.

6.3 TOSTRING

Description:

The TOSTRING function in Tableau is used for type conversion, specifically for converting a field or expression to a string data type. This function is valuable when you need to change the data type of a field from another type, such as a number, to a string.

Syntax:

The syntax for the TOSTRING function is straightforward:

```
```

TOSTRING(expression)

```
```

- `expression`: This is the field or expression that you want to convert to a string.

Example Usage:

Suppose you have a dataset with a field named "Age" stored as integers, and you want to convert it to strings:

```tableau
TOSTRING([Age])
```

Explanation of the Code:

- In this example, the TOSTRING function is applied to the "Age" field. It takes the integer values in the "Age" field and converts them into string values. The result is a field with numeric values represented as strings.

Tips:

1. Use TOSTRING when you need to change the data type of a field to a string.

2. Ensure that the values in the field you're converting can be validly represented as strings. The conversion will work for numeric values, but may not be suitable for non-numeric data, such as dates or non-numeric characters.

3. Be cautious when performing calculations or comparisons with fields after conversion to strings, as the string representation may affect the results.

VII.
Financial Functions

7.1 NPV

Description:

The NPV (Net Present Value) function in Tableau is used for financial analysis and is commonly used to evaluate the profitability of an investment or project over time. It calculates the present value of a series of future cash flows, considering a specific discount rate.

Syntax:

The syntax for the NPV function is as follows:

```
```

NPV(rate, cashflow1, cashflow2, ...)

```
```

- `rate`: This is the discount rate used to discount future cash flows back to their present value.

- `cashflow1`, `cashflow2`, ...: These are the individual cash flows at different time periods, typically representing costs and benefits associated with the investment or project.

Example Usage:

Let's consider a simple investment project. You invest $1,000 in Year 0, and you receive $400 in Year 1, $500 in Year 2, and $600 in Year 3. The discount rate is 5%.

```tableau
```

```
NPV(0.05, -1000, 400, 500, 600)
```

Explanation of the Code:

- In this example, we calculate the Net Present Value of an investment with a discount rate of 5%. The initial investment in Year 0 is -$1,000, which is an outflow (negative value). In Year 1, you receive $400, which is an inflow (positive value). Similarly, there are inflows of $500 and $600 in Years 2 and 3, respectively. The NPV function calculates the present value of these cash flows and returns a single value representing the net present value of the investment.

Tips:

1. Ensure that the discount rate you use in the NPV function is appropriate for the context. The discount rate is a critical factor in the NPV calculation and can significantly impact the results.

2. NPV is a standard financial metric used to assess the attractiveness of investments. A positive NPV suggests that the investment is expected to be profitable, while a negative NPV indicates the investment is not financially sound.

3. Use consistent time periods for cash flows. In the example, cash flows were yearly, and the discount rate was annual. Make sure to match the time periods for accurate calculations.

7.2 IRR

Description:

The IRR (Internal Rate of Return) function in Tableau is used for financial analysis and is a method to evaluate the profitability of an investment or project. It calculates the discount rate at which the Net Present Value (NPV) of a series of future cash flows becomes zero. In other words, IRR is the interest rate at which the investment breaks even.

Syntax:

The syntax for the IRR function is as follows:

```
IRR(cashflow1, cashflow2, ...)
```

- `cashflow1`, `cashflow2`, ...: These are the individual cash flows at different time periods, typically representing costs and benefits associated with the investment or project.

Example Usage:

Let's consider a simple investment project. You invest $1,000 in Year 0, and you receive $400 in Year 1, $500 in Year 2, and $600 in Year 3.

```tableau
IRR(-1000, 400, 500, 600)
```

Explanation of the Code:

- In this example, we calculate the Internal Rate of Return (IRR) for an investment. The initial investment in Year 0 is -$1,000, which is an outflow (negative value). In Year 1, you receive

$400, which is an inflow (positive value). Similarly, there are inflows of $500 and $600 in Years 2 and 3, respectively. The IRR function finds the interest rate at which the Net Present Value of these cash flows becomes zero.

Tips:

1. IRR is a valuable metric for assessing the attractiveness of investments. A higher IRR typically indicates a more profitable investment.

2. When using the IRR function, make sure the project's cash flows are periodic and represent a clear pattern, such as regular investments and returns.

3. Be aware that IRR may have multiple solutions or may not converge in some cases. It's crucial to interpret the result in the context of your specific investment.

4. Be cautious when comparing IRR across projects or investments, as it may not always provide a clear ranking of profitability, especially when dealing with non-conventional cash flows. In such cases, use IRR in conjunction with other financial metrics like NPV for a more comprehensive analysis.

Description:

The FV (Future Value) function in Tableau is used for financial calculations. It calculates the future value of an investment or loan based on a fixed interest rate and consistent payments over a specified period.

Syntax:

The syntax for the FV function is as follows:

```
```

FV(rate, nper, pmt, [pv], [type])

```
```

- `rate`: The interest rate for each period.

- `nper`: The total number of payment periods.

- `pmt`: The periodic payment amount (annuity).

- `pv` (optional): The present value or principal amount of the loan or investment. It is typically omitted and assumed to be zero.

- `type` (optional): Indicates whether payments are made at the beginning or end of each period (0 for end of the period, 1 for the beginning). It is typically omitted and assumed to be 0.

Example Usage:

Suppose you're making monthly deposits of $500 into a savings account that earns an annual interest rate of 4%, and you want to calculate how much money you will have in the account after 5 years.

```tableau
FV(0.04/12, 5*12, -500)
```

Explanation of the Code:

- In this example, we calculate the future value of monthly deposits. We divide the annual interest rate (4%) by 12 to get the monthly rate. The total number of payments is calculated by multiplying the number of years (5) by 12 months. The periodic payment amount is -$500 (a deposit is an inflow, hence the negative value). We omit the present value and type parameters, assuming the default values.

Tips:

1. The FV function is commonly used for retirement planning, savings goals, and investment projections.

2. Be consistent with the units of rate and time (e.g., if the rate is annual, the number of periods should be in years, and the payment should match the period frequency).

3. Ensure that signs are used correctly; for instance, investments or savings are usually positive, and loans are negative.

4. If the payment type (beginning or end of the period) is important for your financial analysis, specify it explicitly using the type parameter.

Description:

The PV (Present Value) function in Tableau is used for financial calculations. It calculates the present value of an investment or loan based on a fixed interest rate, future value, and the number of periods.

Syntax:

The syntax for the PV function is as follows:

```
```

PV(rate, nper, pmt, [fv], [type])

```
```

- `rate`: The interest rate for each period.

- `nper`: The total number of payment periods.

- `pmt`: The periodic payment amount (annuity).

- `fv` (optional): The future value or desired cash balance after the last payment is made. It is typically omitted and assumed to be zero.

- `type` (optional): Indicates whether payments are made at the beginning or end of each period (0 for end of the period, 1 for the beginning). It is typically omitted and assumed to be 0.

Example Usage:

Suppose you want to determine how much you should invest today in order to have $100,000 in 10 years, given an annual interest rate of 5%.

```tableau
PV(0.05, 10, 0, 100000)
```

Explanation of the Code:

- In this example, we calculate the present value needed to reach a future value of $100,000. The annual interest rate is 5%, and the number of years is 10. There are no periodic payments (annuity), so the pmt parameter is 0. We specify the future value as $100,000, and the default type is used, assuming payments are made at the end of each period.

Tips:

1. The PV function is commonly used to determine the initial investment required for savings, loans, or other financial goals.

2. Be consistent with the units of rate and time (e.g., if the rate is annual, the number of periods should be in years).

3. Ensure that signs are used correctly; future values are typically positive, while investments are negative.

4. If the payment type (beginning or end of the period) is important for your financial analysis, specify it explicitly using the type parameter. l

7.5 RATE

Description:

The RATE function in Tableau is used for financial calculations. It calculates the interest rate per period for an investment or loan given the number of periods, periodic payments, present value, and future value. This function is particularly useful for analyzing loan or investment scenarios.

Syntax:

The syntax for the RATE function is as follows:

```
RATE(nper, pmt, pv, [fv], [type], [guess])
```

- `nper`: The total number of payment periods.

- `pmt`: The periodic payment amount (annuity).

- `pv`: The present value or initial investment.

- `fv` (optional): The future value or desired cash balance after the last payment is made. It is typically omitted and assumed to be zero.

- `type` (optional): Indicates whether payments are made at the beginning or end of each period (0 for end of the period, 1 for the beginning). It is typically omitted and assumed to be 0.

- `guess` (optional): An optional value to provide an initial guess for the interest rate. It is typically omitted or set to 0.1.

Example Usage:

Suppose you have a loan of $10,000, with monthly payments of $500 for 24 months, and you want to find the monthly interest rate.

```tableau
RATE(24, -500, 10000)
```

Explanation of the Code:

- In this example, the RATE function calculates the monthly interest rate required to pay off a $10,000 loan with 24 monthly payments of $500 each. The negative value for the pmt parameter indicates payments being made, and the interest rate is calculated as a monthly rate.

Tips:

1. The RATE function is often used to analyze loans and investment opportunities, helping you understand the interest rates associated with your financial transactions.

2. If you provide an initial guess, it can help the function converge faster when finding the interest rate.

3. Ensure that the signs are used correctly; present values and payment amounts are typically negative for loans or investments.

4. Be consistent with the units of time and payment frequency. If your nper is in months, the rate should be a monthly rate.

Description:

The NPER function in Tableau is a financial function used for calculating the number of periods required to reach a desired investment goal or repay a loan, given the periodic payment, interest rate, present value, and future value. It is useful for financial planning and decision-making, helping to determine the time it takes to achieve a specific financial target.

Syntax:

The syntax for the NPER function is as follows:

```
NPER(rate, pmt, pv, [fv], [type])
```

- `rate`: The interest rate per period.

- `pmt`: The periodic payment amount (annuity).

- `pv`: The present value or initial investment.

- `fv` (optional): The future value or desired cash balance after the last payment is made. It is typically omitted and assumed to be zero.

- `type` (optional): Indicates whether payments are made at the beginning or end of each period (0 for end of the period, 1 for the beginning). It is typically omitted and assumed to be 0.

Example Usage:

Suppose you are planning to invest $5,000 at an annual interest rate of 6%, and you want to know how long it will take to reach a future value of $7,000 with annual payments.

```tableau
NPER(0.06, -1000, 5000, 7000)
```

```
```

Explanation of the Code:

- In this example, the NPER function calculates the number of years it will take to reach a future value of $7,000 with an initial investment of $5,000, annual payments of $1,000, and an annual interest rate of 6%. The negative value for the pmt parameter indicates payments being made.

Tips:

1. The NPER function is useful for understanding the time required to achieve your financial goals or repay loans.

2. Ensure consistency in units of time and payment frequency. If the rate is an annual rate, make sure the payment and time are also in years.

3. Use the correct signs for cash flows. Typically, investments are considered as positive cash flows, and payments or loans are negative cash flows.

4. Understand the meaning of each parameter in the context of your financial problem to use the function correctly.

VIII.
Geographic Functions

8.1 DISTANCE

Description:

The DISTANCE function in Tableau is used to calculate the distance between two geographical points (latitude and longitude) on the Earth's surface. It helps analyze and visualize spatial data, allowing you to measure the distance between locations.

Syntax:

The syntax for the DISTANCE function is as follows:

```sql
DISTANCE(latitude1, longitude1, latitude2, longitude2 [, "unit"])
```

- `latitude1`: The latitude of the first point.

- `longitude1`: The longitude of the first point.

- `latitude2`: The latitude of the second point.

- `longitude2`: The longitude of the second point.

- `"unit"` (optional): The unit of measurement for the distance (default is "miles" if not specified). Possible units are "miles," "kilometers," "meters," "feet," "yards," and more.

Example Usage:

Suppose you want to calculate the distance between two cities with the following coordinates:

- City A: Latitude 34.0522, Longitude -118.2437

- City B: Latitude 40.7128, Longitude -74.0060

```sql
DISTANCE(34.0522, -118.2437, 40.7128, -74.0060, "miles")
```

Explanation of the Code:

- In this example, the DISTANCE function calculates the distance between City A and City B. The result will be in miles because the "unit" parameter is specified as "miles."

Tips:

1. Make sure you have the correct latitude and longitude values for the locations you want to calculate the distance between.

2. Be consistent with the unit of measurement; use a unit that makes sense for your analysis and visualization.

3. Consider rounding the results to a reasonable number of decimal places to improve readability and interpretation.

4. When using the DISTANCE function, ensure you have the necessary spatial data or location data available in your dataset.

8.2 INTERSECTS

Description:

The INTERSECTS function in Tableau is used to check whether two geographical shapes or objects intersect with each other. It helps in spatial analysis by determining if two geographic objects overlap or have any common area of intersection. This is particularly useful when working with geographic data such as maps.

Syntax:

The syntax for the INTERSECTS function is as follows:

```sql
INTERSECTS(Geometry1, Geometry2)
```

- `Geometry1`: The first geographic object or shape.
- `Geometry2`: The second geographic object or shape.

Example Usage:

Suppose you have a dataset with geographic data representing polygons of two regions, and you want to identify if these two regions intersect.

```sql
INTERSECTS([Region1], [Region2])
```

Explanation of the Code:

- In this example, the INTERSECTS function checks whether the polygon representing Region1 intersects with the polygon representing Region2. If there is any common area between the two polygons, it will return TRUE; otherwise, it will return FALSE.

Tips:

1. Ensure that your dataset contains appropriate geographic data with valid shapes or geometries for this function to work correctly.

2. You can use the INTERSECTS function in combination with other functions or conditions to perform more complex spatial analyses.

3. Remember that the result of the INTERSECTS function is a Boolean value (TRUE or FALSE), which can be used for filtering or creating calculated fields in your Tableau visualizations.

4. When working with geographic data, consider the coordinate systems and projections used, as they can impact the accuracy of intersection calculations.

8.3 WITHIN

Description:

The WITHIN function in Tableau is used to check whether one geographic shape or object is completely within another. This function is essential for spatial analysis when working with geographic data and maps, as it helps identify containment relationships between geographic objects.

Syntax:

The syntax for the WITHIN function is as follows:

```sql
WITHIN(Geometry1, Geometry2)
```

- `Geometry1`: The geographic object or shape that you want to check if it is within another.

- `Geometry2`: The geographic object or shape that serves as the reference for containment.

Example Usage:

Suppose you have a dataset with geographic data representing various regions and want to determine if a specific point is within a particular polygon representing a region.

```sql
WITHIN([Point], [Region])
```

Explanation of the Code:

- In this example, the WITHIN function checks whether the point represented by [Point] is within the polygon represented by [Region]. If the point is entirely contained within the polygon, it returns TRUE; otherwise, it returns FALSE.

Tips:

1. Ensure that your dataset contains valid geographic data with appropriate shapes or geometries for the WITHIN function to work accurately.

2. You can use the WITHIN function in combination with other spatial functions or conditions to perform more complex geographic analyses.

3. When dealing with geographic data in Tableau, consider the coordinate systems, projections, and spatial units to ensure consistent and accurate results.

4. The result of the WITHIN function is a Boolean value (TRUE or FALSE), which you can use for filtering, calculated fields, or spatial visualizations in Tableau.

8.4 GEOALIAS

Description:

The GEOALIAS function in Tableau is used to create an alias for a geographic dimension. It allows you to assign a user-friendly name to geographic values while maintaining the original values for data mapping and analysis. This function is useful when you want to display more descriptive or customized geographic labels on maps.

Syntax:

The syntax for the GEOALIAS function is as follows:

```sql
GEOALIAS(GeographicField, Alias)
```

- `GeographicField`: The geographic dimension or field that you want to assign an alias to.

- `Alias`: The user-defined alias or custom label that you want to display instead of the original values.

Example Usage:

Suppose you have a dataset containing a geographic field named "Country" with full country names, but you want to create custom abbreviations for these countries for map labels.

```sql
GEOALIAS([Country], "USA", "United States of America")
```

Explanation of the Code:

- In this example, the GEOALIAS function assigns the alias "USA" to the value "United States of America" in the "Country" field. When used in Tableau visualizations, "United States of America" will be displayed as "USA" on the map.

Tips:

1. The GEOALIAS function is particularly helpful when you want to display more concise or user-friendly labels on maps while keeping the original values intact for data analysis.

2. You can use GEOALIAS in combination with other geographic functions and parameters to enhance your spatial visualizations and improve data interpretation.

3. Make sure the aliases you define are consistent and meaningful for your audience to understand the geographic context of your data.

4. You can use GEOALIAS in calculated fields and calculated dimensions to apply aliases dynamically based on specific conditions or rules.

5. Keep in mind that aliasing does not change the underlying data; it only affects how data is displayed in visualizations.

8.5 GEOCODE

Description:

The `GEOCODE` function in Tableau is used to perform geocoding, which is the process of converting textual location data into geographic coordinates (latitude and longitude) that can be plotted on maps. This function is helpful when you have location data in your dataset but need to visualize it on a map. By using the `GEOCODE` function, you can accurately map data points and create compelling geographical visualizations in Tableau.

Syntax:

The syntax for the `GEOCODE` function in Tableau is as follows:

```tableau
GEOCODE(string_expression)
```

- `string_expression`: This is a string or dimension that represents a location or address you want to geocode.

Example Usage:

Let's consider a scenario where you have a dataset with a column named "City" that contains the names of cities. You want to geocode these city names to latitude and longitude coordinates for mapping. You can use the `GEOCODE` function as follows:

```tableau
GEOCODE([City])
```

In this example, `[City]` is a dimension that represents the city names you want to geocode.

Explanation:

1. `GEOCODE([City])` takes each city name from the "City" column in your dataset and sends it to the Tableau geocoding service.

2. The geocoding service processes the city names and returns the corresponding latitude and longitude coordinates.

Tips:

- Ensure that you have a reliable internet connection when using the `GEOCODE` function because it relies on an online geocoding service provided by Tableau.

- Verify that the city names or addresses in your dataset are accurate and correctly formatted to improve geocoding accuracy.

- Check your Tableau settings to ensure that the geocoding service is properly configured.

- You can customize how geocoded data is displayed on maps in Tableau, including setting the map style and colors.

Using the `GEOCODE` function, you can turn your location data into meaningful visualizations on maps, providing a better understanding of spatial relationships within your data.

8.6 AREA

Description:

The AREA function in Tableau is used to calculate the area of geographic shapes or polygons in a spatial field. It allows you to quantify the size of geographic regions or objects on a map, which can be useful for spatial analysis and data visualization. The calculated area is typically in square units relevant to the spatial reference of the data, such as square meters, square kilometers, or square miles.

Syntax:

The syntax for the AREA function is as follows:

```sql
AREA(GeographicField)
```

- `GeographicField`: The geographic field or spatial object for which you want to calculate the area.

Example Usage:

Suppose you have a dataset that contains a spatial field named "Polygon" representing different land parcels. You want to calculate the area of each land parcel.

```sql
AREA([Polygon])
```

Explanation of the Code:

- In this example, the AREA function calculates the area of each polygon in the "Polygon" field. The result will provide the area of each land parcel in the unit of measurement relevant to the spatial data.

Tips:

1. The AREA function is particularly useful for geographic and spatial analysis. It helps in understanding the size and scale of geographic features.

2. Ensure that your spatial data has a proper spatial reference system (SRS) set up to get accurate area calculations in appropriate units.

3. Be aware that the units of measurement for area calculations will depend on the spatial reference of your data. Make sure to document and communicate the units you are using in your visualizations.

4. Use the AREA function in combination with other spatial functions and dimensions to create insightful geographic visualizations and calculations.

5. Be cautious when dealing with extremely small or large polygons, as these might result in very small or very large area values, which could impact your visualizations. Consider scaling or transforming the data when necessary.

8.7 POINT

Description:

The POINT function in Tableau is used to create a point geometry or spatial object within a spatial field. This allows you to define a specific location in geographic coordinates, and it's often used to mark a single point on a map. You can use this function to specify latitude and longitude values for a point or to transform other data into geographic points.

Syntax:

The syntax for the POINT function is as follows:

```sql
POINT(Latitude, Longitude)
```

- `Latitude`: The latitude value for the point.
- `Longitude`: The longitude value for the point.

Example Usage:

Suppose you have a dataset with latitude and longitude columns and want to create a point geometry based on these coordinates.

```sql
POINT([Latitude], [Longitude])
```

Explanation of the Code:

- In this example, the POINT function is used to create a point geometry based on the latitude and longitude values from the "Latitude" and "Longitude" columns. The result is a point object that represents a specific location on a map.

Tips:

1. The POINT function is useful when you need to visualize specific geographic coordinates or locations on a map.

2. Ensure that your latitude and longitude values are correctly formatted, and they represent valid geographic coordinates.

3. You can use this function in combination with other spatial functions to create more complex spatial objects or perform spatial calculations.

4. When working with latitude and longitude values, make sure they are in the appropriate coordinate system (e.g., WGS 84), which is commonly used for mapping applications.

5. Verify that your data source provides accurate latitude and longitude information for meaningful use of the POINT function in your visualizations.

IX.
Set Functions

9.1 SET

Description:

The SET function in Tableau allows you to create a set, which is a custom subset of data based on specified conditions. Sets are useful for creating customized groups of data points, and they are often used for further analysis or visualization in Tableau.

Syntax:

The syntax for the SET function is as follows:

```sql
SET [Set Name] AS [Condition]
```

- `Set Name`: The name you want to give to the set.
- `Condition`: The condition or criteria for defining the set.

Example Usage:

Suppose you have a dataset of sales data and you want to create a set of high-value customers who have made purchases over $1,000.

```sql
```

```
SET HighValueCustomers AS [Sales] > 1000
```

Explanation of the Code:

- In this example, a set named "HighValueCustomers" is created.

- The condition `[Sales] > 1000` is used to define the set. This condition selects all rows where the "Sales" column has a value greater than $1,000.

- The set "HighValueCustomers" now contains all the data points (rows) that meet this condition.

Tips:

1. Sets are dynamic in Tableau, meaning they update automatically as your data changes or filters are applied.

2. You can use sets to group data points together for further analysis, such as creating custom aggregations or visualizations.

3. Sets can be based on conditions involving multiple columns or dimensions, providing flexibility in defining subsets of data.

4. Sets are particularly useful in creating complex filters or for segmenting data to compare different subsets.

5. Sets can be combined with other sets using set operations (union, intersect, etc.) to create even more advanced data groupings.

6. Sets can be used in calculated fields, parameters, and visualizations to control and customize how data is displayed.

9.2 ISMEMBER

Description:

The ISMEMBER function in Tableau is used to check if a data point belongs to a specific set. A set is a custom subset of data created in Tableau. ISMEMBER returns a Boolean value (TRUE or FALSE) based on whether the data point is a member of the specified set.

Syntax:

The syntax for the ISMEMBER function is as follows:

```sql
ISMEMBER('Set Name')
```

- `'Set Name'`: The name of the set you want to check membership for.

Example Usage:

Suppose you have created a set named "HighValueCustomers," and you want to check if a particular customer belongs to this set.

```sql
ISMEMBER('HighValueCustomers')
```

Explanation of the Code:

- The ISMEMBER function is used to check if the data point belongs to the "HighValueCustomers" set.

- If the data point is a member of the set, the function returns TRUE. Otherwise, it returns FALSE.

Tips:

1. ISMEMBER is useful when you want to perform conditional actions or filtering based on whether a data point belongs to a particular set.

2. You can use ISMEMBER within calculated fields to create custom logic or aggregations based on set membership.

3. Combine ISMEMBER with other functions to create complex conditions and control the display or behavior of your Tableau visualizations.

4. ISMEMBER is especially valuable for creating dynamic interactive dashboards, where users can select sets or subsets of data to view.

9.3 ISNULL

Description:

The ISNULL function in Tableau is used to check whether a field or expression contains a null (missing) value. It returns a Boolean value (TRUE or FALSE) based on whether the specified field or expression contains a null value. Null values represent missing or undefined data in your dataset.

Syntax:

The syntax for the ISNULL function is as follows:

```sql
ISNULL(expression)
```

- `expression`: The field or expression you want to check for null values.

Example Usage:

Suppose you have a field named "Sales" and you want to check if it contains any null values.

```sql
ISNULL([Sales])
```

Explanation of the Code:

- The ISNULL function checks if the "Sales" field contains null values.

- If the field contains any null values, the function returns TRUE. Otherwise, it returns FALSE.

Tips:

1. ISNULL is useful for data cleansing and validation. You can quickly identify and handle missing data points in your dataset.

2. You can combine ISNULL with other Tableau functions to create more complex logic. For example, you might use ISNULL with IF to perform conditional actions based on null values.

3. When working with databases and SQL data sources, ISNULL can be used to handle database NULL values and transform them into more meaningful representations.

4. Be cautious when using ISNULL, as it checks for the presence of null values. If you need to check for empty strings or zero values, consider using other functions like IFNULL or ZN.

9.4 ATTR

Description:

The ATTR function in Tableau is used to retrieve a single value for an attribute from a dimension. It returns the unique value of an attribute for a given dimension member. This function is particularly useful when you're working with dimensions that have been aggregated or transformed, and you want to access the original attribute value.

Syntax:

The syntax for the ATTR function is as follows:

```sql
ATTR(attribute)
```

- `attribute`: The dimension attribute for which you want to retrieve the value.

Example Usage:

Suppose you have a dataset with a dimension called "Product Category" and an associated attribute "Product Name." You want to retrieve the product name for a specific category, like "Electronics."

```sql
ATTR([Product Name])
```

Explanation of the Code:

- The ATTR function retrieves the value of the "Product Name" attribute for the selected dimension member (in this case, "Electronics").

- It will return the unique product name associated with the "Electronics" category.

Tips:

1. Use the ATTR function when you need to access the specific attribute value of a dimension, especially in situations where the dimension has been aggregated or grouped.

2. ATTR can be used in calculated fields to create custom aggregations or calculations based on dimension attributes.

3. Be cautious when using ATTR, as it should be used with dimensions that have a one-to-one relationship with their attributes. If there is a many-to-one relationship, ATTR may not return the expected results.

4. If you want to retrieve the first attribute value for a dimension member in a visualization, consider using the FIRST() function.

5. When combining ATTR with other functions, ensure that you're working with the appropriate level of detail to get the desired results.

9.5 UNION

Description:

The UNION function in Tableau is used to combine data from multiple data sources or tables into a single result set. It's particularly helpful when you have data that is spread across different tables or files and need to bring them together for analysis. Union operations can be performed on data with similar structures.

Syntax:

The syntax for the UNION function is as follows:

```sql
UNION [ALL]
```

- `ALL` (optional): When specified, it includes all rows from both tables, even if they are duplicates. If not specified, duplicate rows are eliminated.

Example Usage:

Suppose you have two tables, `Sales2022` and `Sales2023`, with similar structures, and you want to combine their data into a single result set.

```sql
SELECT * FROM Sales2022
UNION
SELECT * FROM Sales2023
```

Explanation of the Code:

- The UNION operation combines the rows from the `Sales2022` and `Sales2023` tables into a single result set.

- By default, duplicate rows are removed, so you get a unique set of rows. If you want to include duplicates, you can use `UNION ALL` instead.

Tips:

1. Ensure that the tables or data sources you are attempting to union have similar structures, including the same columns and data types.

2. UNION is a useful function for creating consolidated datasets from different sources or tables for analysis or reporting purposes.

3. Be cautious when using UNION, especially when dealing with large datasets, as it can result in a significant increase in the number of rows in the result set.

4. Pay attention to the order of columns in the SELECT statements. The columns' order in the result set will follow the order in the first SELECT statement.

5. UNION can also be used in combination with other operations like JOINs to merge data from various sources based on specific criteria.

9.6 INTERSECT

Description:

The INTERSECT function in Tableau is used to retrieve the common records from two different result sets, such as the result of two separate SELECT statements. It returns only the rows that appear in both result sets, effectively finding the intersection of data.

Syntax:

The syntax for the INTERSECT function is as follows:

```sql
SELECT column1, column2, ...

FROM table1

INTERSECT

SELECT column1, column2, ...

FROM table2;
```

Example Usage:

Suppose you have two tables, `Customers` and `Orders`, and you want to find the customers who have placed orders. You can use the INTERSECT function to find common records between these two tables.

```sql
SELECT CustomerName

FROM Customers

INTERSECT
```

```
SELECT CustomerName

FROM Orders;

```

Explanation of the Code:

- The INTERSECT operation combines the results of two SELECT statements to find records that exist in both the `Customers` and `Orders` tables.

- In this case, it retrieves the names of customers who have placed orders, ensuring that only common records are returned.

Tips:

1. Make sure the columns and data types in the SELECT statements are consistent, as INTERSECT requires the same column structure in both SELECT statements.

2. INTERSECT is an effective way to find common records between two sets, useful for data validation, identifying shared elements, or other situations where you need to compare data.

3. Note that INTERSECT returns distinct rows. If there are duplicate rows in either of the source tables, they will be counted only once in the result set.

4. If you want to find the records that are unique to each result set, you can use the EXCEPT or LEFT JOIN/RIGHT JOIN operators in combination with INTERSECT.

5. Be cautious with the performance of INTERSECT, especially when working with large datasets, as it requires processing and comparison of both result sets.

9.7 DIFFERENCE

Description:

The DIFFERENCE function in Tableau is used to calculate the difference between two sets or results of two separate SELECT statements. It returns the records that exist in the first result set but not in the second, effectively finding the difference between data sets.

Syntax:

The syntax for the DIFFERENCE function is as follows:

```sql
SELECT column1, column2, ...
FROM table1
DIFFERENCE
SELECT column1, column2, ...
FROM table2;
```

Example Usage:

Suppose you have two tables, `Students` and `Graduates`, and you want to find the students who have not yet graduated. You can use the DIFFERENCE function to find the records that exist in the `Students` table but not in the `Graduates` table.

```sql
SELECT StudentName
FROM Students
DIFFERENCE
```

```
SELECT StudentName

FROM Graduates;
```

Explanation of the Code:

- The DIFFERENCE operation combines the results of two SELECT statements to find records that exist in the first table but not in the second.

- In this case, it retrieves the names of students who have not yet graduated, ensuring that only the unique records are returned.

Tips:

1. Ensure that the columns and data types in the SELECT statements are consistent, as DIFFERENCE requires the same column structure in both SELECT statements.

2. DIFFERENCE is useful for finding records that are unique to the first result set, making it valuable for data validation or identifying records that don't meet certain criteria.

3. Be cautious with the performance of DIFFERENCE, especially when working with large datasets, as it requires processing and comparison of both result sets.

4. If you want to find records that are common to both result sets, you can use the INTERSECT operator in combination with DIFFERENCE.

5. If you are dealing with large datasets or complex queries, ensure that you have appropriate indexing and performance optimizations in place for efficient query execution.

X.
User Functions

10.1 USERNAME

Description:

The USERNAME function in Tableau is used to retrieve the name of the currently logged-in user. It returns the username or login name of the user who is accessing or interacting with the Tableau workbook or dashboard.

Syntax:

The USERNAME function is a simple function with no required syntax. It is used directly in calculated fields or calculated expressions to retrieve the username. For example:

```
USERNAME()
```

Example Usage:

Suppose you have a dashboard that displays a welcome message based on the currently logged-in user. You can use the USERNAME function to dynamically fetch the username.

```sql
"Welcome, " + USERNAME()
```

Explanation of the Code:

- The `USERNAME()` function is used to retrieve the username of the currently logged-in user.

- It is then combined with the "Welcome, " text to create a dynamic message that greets the user by their name.

Tips:

1. The USERNAME function is most commonly used in calculated fields or calculated expressions within Tableau worksheets or dashboards.

2. It's useful for personalizing content or greetings in dashboards, reports, or visualizations based on the currently logged-in user.

3. Ensure that user authentication and security settings are properly configured in your Tableau environment to make use of the USERNAME function.

4. USERNAME() returns the username as a string, so you can use it in combination with other text or functions as needed for your specific use case.

5. Always be mindful of data security and privacy when using user-specific information.

10.2 USEREMAIL

Description:

The USEREMAIL function in Tableau is used to retrieve the email address of the currently logged-in user. It returns the email address associated with the user who is accessing or interacting with the Tableau workbook or dashboard. This function is helpful when you need to incorporate user-specific email information into your visualizations or calculations.

Syntax:

The USEREMAIL function is straightforward to use. It doesn't require any parameters or syntax. You can directly use it in calculated fields or calculated expressions to fetch the user's email address. For example:

```
USEREMAIL()
```

Example Usage:

Suppose you have a dashboard that includes a "Contact Us" button. When a user clicks the button, it should open an email window addressed to the currently logged-in user. You can use the USEREMAIL function to achieve this.

```sql
"mailto:" + USEREMAIL()
```

Explanation of the Code:

- The `USEREMAIL()` function retrieves the email address of the currently logged-in user.

- The email address is combined with the "mailto:" prefix, creating a hyperlink. When the user clicks this link, it opens their default email client, pre-filled with their email address.

Tips:

1. The USEREMAIL function is commonly used in calculated fields or calculated expressions within Tableau worksheets or dashboards.

2. It's useful for personalizing interactions, such as providing contact options based on the user's email.

3. Ensure that user authentication and security settings are properly configured in your Tableau environment to make use of the USEREMAIL function.

4. USEREMAIL() returns the email address as a string, allowing you to use it in combination with other text or functions as needed for your specific use case.

5. Be mindful of data security and privacy when using user-specific information, especially email addresses.

10.3 USERGROUP

Description:

The USERGROUP function in Tableau is used to retrieve information about the groups that the currently logged-in user belongs to. It allows you to access and work with group membership data, which is especially useful for creating user-specific content or applying security rules based on user groups.

Syntax:

The USERGROUP function does not require any parameters. It is used as follows:

```
USERGROUP()
```

Example Usage:

Let's say you have a Tableau dashboard with different sections, each intended for a specific user group. You want to display only the section corresponding to the user's group. You can achieve this using the USERGROUP function in combination with an IF statement.

```sql
IF USERGROUP() = 'Admin Group' THEN 'Admin Dashboard'

ELSEIF USERGROUP() = 'Sales Group' THEN 'Sales Dashboard'

ELSE 'General Dashboard'

END
```

```
```

Explanation of the Code:

- The `USERGROUP()` function retrieves the user's group information.

- An `IF` statement checks the user's group and returns the corresponding dashboard name based on the group membership.

- If the user is a member of the "Admin Group," they see the "Admin Dashboard." If they belong to the "Sales Group," they see the "Sales Dashboard." Otherwise, they see the "General Dashboard."

Tips:

1. The USERGROUP function is valuable when you need to customize content or security rules based on user groups.

2. User groups in Tableau are often defined and managed in your organization's authentication system, such as Active Directory or LDAP.

3. Be careful when using USERGROUP data, as it may expose sensitive information about your users and their roles.

4. Always ensure proper authentication and security configurations to accurately retrieve group data in Tableau.

5. Use the returned user group information to dynamically control what content or data users can access, making your Tableau dashboards more user-specific and secure.

10.4 USERID

Description:

The USERID function in Tableau is used to retrieve information about the currently logged-in user's unique identifier. It returns a unique identifier associated with the user, which can be used for various purposes, such as tracking user actions, creating user-specific content, or for data security.

Syntax:

The USERID function does not require any parameters. It is used as follows:

```
USERID()
```

Example Usage:

Suppose you want to create a log that tracks user interactions with your Tableau dashboard, recording which users make changes to a parameter. You can use the USERID function to capture the unique user identifier in a data source.

```sql
IF [Parameter Change] = TRUE THEN USERID() ELSE NULL END
```

Explanation of the Code:

- The `USERID()` function retrieves the unique user identifier.

- An `IF` statement checks if a parameter change has occurred (assuming there's a boolean field `[Parameter Change]`).

- If a parameter change is detected, the `USERID()` value is recorded in the log; otherwise, it's set to NULL.

Tips:

1. The USERID function can be useful for auditing and tracking user actions within your Tableau dashboards or reports.

2. This function provides a way to uniquely identify users without revealing sensitive information.

3. The USERID is specific to the Tableau environment and is not a user's personal or external identifier.

4. Ensure that proper data security and privacy measures are in place when using USERID to avoid any misuse of user-related data.

5. The USERID can also be used to filter data based on the currently logged-in user, ensuring they only see data relevant to them.

10.5 USERROLE

Description:

The USERROLE function in Tableau is used to retrieve information about the currently logged-in user's role or group membership. It allows you to check the role or group of a user and make decisions based on their role. This function is often used in security or conditional logic scenarios to display content or data specific to certain roles or groups.

Syntax:

The USERROLE function does not require any parameters. It is used as follows:

```
USERROLE()
```

Example Usage:

Suppose you have a Tableau dashboard that contains sensitive financial data, and you want to restrict access to this data based on a user's role. You can use the USERROLE function to determine a user's role and filter the data accordingly.

```sql
IF USERROLE() = 'Admin' THEN [Financial Data] ELSE NULL END
```

Explanation of the Code:

- The `USERROLE()` function retrieves the role or group of the currently logged-in user.

- An `IF` statement checks if the user's role is 'Admin' (assuming 'Admin' is a valid role in your system).

- If the user is an admin, they can access the financial data; otherwise, the data is set to NULL.

Tips:

1. USERROLE is a valuable function for implementing role-based security in your Tableau dashboards.

2. It can help control what specific users or groups can see or interact with in your reports.

3. Make sure that the roles or groups you are checking with USERROLE are well-defined and maintained within your Tableau environment.

4. USERROLE values are case-sensitive. Be consistent with the case (e.g., 'Admin' and 'admin' are treated as different roles).

5. Test your security logic thoroughly to ensure it provides the desired access control while maintaining good performance.

CONCLUSION

In conclusion, Tableau offers a robust set of functions and capabilities that empower users to analyze and visualize data efficiently. These functions enable users to perform complex calculations, manipulate data, and create custom time periods for in-depth analysis. Understanding and effectively using these functions can significantly enhance your data analysis and reporting skills in Tableau.

As you explore the world of data analysis with Tableau, you will discover the power and flexibility of these functions, enabling you to gain insights from your data, make data-driven decisions, and present your findings through compelling visualizations.

We hope that this guide has provided you with valuable insights into some of Tableau's key functions and their usage. We encourage you to explore these functions further and experiment with them in your data analysis projects.

Thank you for choosing our guide.

We sincerely appreciate your support, and we hope that this resource has been helpful on your journey to becoming a Tableau expert. If you have any more questions or need further assistance, please feel free to reach out. Happy analyzing, and may your data adventures be successful and rewarding!